HOW TO KNIT AN OPERA

CHLOE RAYBAN

Published by Ours et Ourson
June 2015
ISBN 9781326086220
'Ours et Ourson' is an independent publisher specialising in non-fiction (biography, travel) and poetry. For more information, go to
www.oursetourson.com

How to Knit an Opera © Chloë Rayban
June 2015

"I often think about you and Peter. You were some of the first people to help create my love for opera and help my career, so I have a lot to thank you for!"
Donna

Chapter One

Someone's asking for a bucket for Count Almaviva to be sick in, she thinks he may have sunstroke. The pianist is sitting on the sofa, he's ostensibly naked apart from a single earring, knitting. Both my hands are covered in cold salmon and the first members of the audience (rather dull and conventional ones) are starting to arrive. How did I get into a mess like this?

The answer is going to take us a long way back. So far that this book risks getting like Tristram Shandy and we might never reach Opera Loki's debut performance. But here goes.

We'd always loved opera. Not in the pretentious way of knowing all performers and performances and one-upping each other on their star ratings. No just loving it for its story-telling and divine music and the way the human voice conveys emotion that speaks directly to the soul. We'd lived in London where opera is readily available as long as you have the cash. We'd queued for returns at Covent Garden, sat up in the gods, or sometimes in the stalls when 'crumbs from the Chairman's table' came our way. Peter worked for an advertising agency where occasionally some lucky employee had to accompany clients to gala opera evenings when the Chairman wasn't available. Treasured tickets for Glyndebourne were similar freebies or otherwise we'd catch up with the Glyndebourne Touring Opera when it went round Britain. For a while Peter worked on the marketing committee for English National Opera and we were given magical complimentary tickets for first nights. Later we both gave voluntary help to attract advertising in Covent Garden programmes and were rewarded with tickets for dress rehearsals. These generally took place in the mornings where we learned the advantage of being wide awake and alert in a way one never is in the evening. We'd be surrounded by lovely ladies from Tonbridge Wells and Esher with their thermos's and sandwiches, who'd come up to Town for the day. And when none of these freebies was available we'd stood at the back of the auditorium till our legs gave out and we went for a consolatory spaghetti across the road at Bertorelli's.

But as fate had it, we had to leave London and the move we made to a remote part of Central France could hardly be further from an Opera House.

Why France? We'd always loved big, old houses. Particularly big old houses in France – where there are a lot of them and they're far cheaper than big old houses in England. You can get an averagely large chateau in France for the price of a country cottage in the Cotswolds. The move to a big old French house came one step closer one Sunday morning, when I was staying with our daughter Claudia in Paris. Peter rang and said, 'I've decided to hand in my notice.' I replied, after a pause to register tactful shock and surprise: 'Go ahead then. We'll manage somehow.' Of course I never thought he'd do it. But he did. So I returned to London to a fifty-five year old unemployed husband and a house in Fulham that was feeling and showing its age.

'Managing somehow', started by turning the spare bedroom into some sort of office for him, as he began to put out feelers for consultancy work. A desk was ordered, British Telecom set to rewiring phone cables all round the doors and I headed up to Peter Jones to buy suitably office-like curtain material. It was in that unlikely environment - the curtain material department of Peter Jones - that the dream really started to take hold. I fingered a deep green woven satin with a dense stripe of burgundy and gold, picturing in my mind how this could be relocated should we ever get what had always been my dream home – that mythical house in France. Four heavy curtain tassels in gold and burgundy and green went into the parcel with the material. Dreams don't come cheap.

No sooner had Peter set foot in his new office than Leo, our younger daughter, announced she had run out of money and wanted to come home and reoccupy her bedroom . She was studying for a Post Grad. Journalism Diploma at City University, so we had a third worker typing away frantically under our roof. Elder daughter Claudia, now a dedicated Parisienne, was already a devotee of Eurostar, reappearing every couple of weekends or so, generally with a Parisian boyfriend in tow. She'd become so good at falling asleep as the train left the Gare du Nord and waking up at Waterloo, she was under the impression that the journey only took half an hour. The 'trophies' she brought home with her, chain-smoked for France and drank all our vodka in their morning fruit juice but did wonders for my schoolgirl French. Then just as we felt the house couldn't get any fuller, we had a call from Peter's father, Leslie. He'd had a fall. Could we drive down to Suffolk and pick him up as he felt he really couldn't cope any more on his own. Another room was made habitable, this time in the basement – luckily we already had a shower room down there, legacy of the au pair our girls had long outgrown.

The house was positively bulging at the seams and then my mother Marjorie started a subtle campaign of invasion. Marjorie it seemed couldn't bear the fact that Leslie was in the house while she lived alone abandoned in Bexhill. Admittedly, she only came for 3-day weekends but this meant that Peter had to vacate his study/spare room and work on his knees in the sitting room. A regime made a little tricky when Leslie made his trip up the stairs for his whisky and the six o'clock news. There was a ritual to the whole thing. Leslie would make his slow progress up the stairs, head for the sitting room window, wait till the six o'clock Concorde had passed overhead, then with a nod to Peter say 'Time to get me a whisky Boy.' With that he'd take possession of the remote control and decide on our viewing options for the evening.
I started to make noises about moving. Carefully timed noises, Peter must of course think the move was his idea. He needed to be relaxed, primed with his evening drink and preferably replete with a nice dinner. Even he could see that we needed to move and to somewhere spacious enough to house our multi-aged ménage. We needed bedrooms and bathrooms on the ground floor for the oldies. Bedrooms on the top floor for the young and maybe a separate sitting room too. A nice suite for us maybe even with our own TV- Leslie proof - somewhere we could escape from the lot of them. But we didn't do anything about it - you always need a catalyst, don't you?

That came one afternoon when I was driving back from my weekly art class. I doubled up over the wheel with stomach cramps. Back home these grew stronger. So strong in fact that a doctor was called and he gave me an injection of pain-killer. I instantly threw up. Fine, I thought, it's just some kind of extreme tummy bug. An hour later I was writhing in agony on the bed, Leo called an ambulance and I ended up in the A&E Department of Chelsea and Westminster Hospital. I was admitted for the night and the pain gradually wore off. Someone came and hung a Nil by Mouth sign over my head. Not a good sign. It seemed I was in for the knife. The next day I felt much better, in fact ready to go home, in spite of the fact I had a stomach like a balloon and was having to pee every half hour.

They wheeled me downstairs for a Cat Scan. I saw the two radiologists put their heads together and overheard one mutter 'There seem to be two of them.' He turned to me, 'You couldn't be pregnant could you?' I replied it was unlikely since I was fifty two and had been sterilised. 'Hmmmm,' he mused.

Back up in the ward again I took stock of my situation. I'd had a skirmish with breast cancer in my 'thirties. So any mention of something alien inside me and ominously 'two of them' rang the panic button. By the next morning I had swapped to the Private Ward since I was on Bupa through Peter's former workplace. In the luxurious gloom and isolation of my private room I decided I'd better come to terms with the fact that I was dying. Whatever it was – or they were – was undoubtedly malignant, so I started taking stock of what I had done in my life. The books I'd had published were a consolation. The two daughters we had - a bonus. But there were the things I hadn't done that lay on my mind like indigestion. Who was going to file my tax statement or explain to anyone else in the house how the central heating worked or what to do when the dishwasher went funny and you had to kick the door to make it start. Who was going to worm the cats and remember everybody's birthdays? These went round and round in my brain. By the next morning I'd started to list these undone things in order of importance. I realised that the one thing I had most wanted to do and never done, was to own that large beautiful house with a garden in France. And the more I thought about this, the more it seemed mad that we hadn't done it. The dream house we hadn't had, would have solved all our problems. But now sadly, it was too late.

That evening a young doctor flung himself through my door and apologised for not coming sooner. It seemed my paperwork had been lost in the move from public to private ward – I was a non-existent patient. He took a look at my bloated stomach, did some pressing and frowning and said he would operate later that night - midnight to be exact. I wondered since I was dying why he couldn't leave it till next morning. At least I could have a last decent night's sleep. But in fact I was so exhausted by the whole thing that after he left I must have fallen asleep. The next thing I knew I was being wheeled down to the operating theatre. I was about to protest – even condemned prisoners are allowed a last wish - when a needle was stuck in my arm.

After that split second in the non-time of anaesthesia, I woke up in the Recovery Room. The nurse was bending over me. 'What was it?' I asked. 'They took out a cyst the size of a grapefruit.,' she said. 'You were very lucky. It was about to burst.'

'Do they think it's cancer?' She shook her head. 'Unlikely, it was full of water.'

I looked up at her in disbelief. Could it be possible that I was going to live?

I'd had a reprieve, a new chance. I was wheeled back up to my room where I lay in a wonderful fuzzy haze of morphine-drugged euphoria building French castles in the air.

When Peter came in to see me next morning, clearly having heard the good news, I greeted him with.

'I've been thinking...'

'Oh yes?'

'I think we ought to move to France.'

He looked back at me expressionlessly while the cogs and wheels of the male brain ground into action.

'Well?'

A slow smile spread across his face. 'We can start looking as soon as you're up and about.'

Chapter Two

When it comes to property – to mis-quote the old adage - the search is far better than the discovery. We had a lot in our favour – we practically owned a large house in a good area of London. Only a fraction of the mortgage was left to pay off. Peter had no job to re-locate, his consultancy work could be done from anywhere with an internet connection. We had no school-age children to educate. Selling up and moving to France made sense. The difference in price between London property and rural France made us literally property millionaires. Incredible as it may seem, property searching in France in 1998 was pre-internet. It was still a time of contacting agents, looking in the Times and the Telegraph and The Lady and the foreign section of property magazines. And then one day we discovered 'Belles Demeures' – a big glossy French publication devoted to large and often eye-wateringly beautiful properties. I scoured the pages like a hunger striker with a five-star menu. Chateaux with moats and witches' hat towers, elegant stuccoed Maisons de Maitre, ancient farmhouses with russet tiled dove-cotes, houses with ponds and fountains, and lakes and avenue upon avenue of trees – and many of these, incredible as it might seem, within our price range.

BUT we'd decided to be sensible about the property – we wouldn't squander everything we had - we needed to keep some sort of flat or pied-a-terre as a foothold in London in case the move didn't work out.

The first decision was the 'departement'. Friends advised Normandy because it was close, the Loire because it was mild - the south because it was hot - the south west because of the mountains – the south east because of the winter sports. However, we had our own agenda. Claudia by now seemed well and truly dug-in in Paris and would want to come for weekends. Peter's principle client was in Switzerland. So we drew a half circle within a 3-4 hour radius south of Paris and concentrated our search round that.

We couldn't simply leave the oldies to fend for themselves so we employed housekeepers to care for young and old while we made our property-finding forays. The housekeepers came from an agency and were expensive. Each of them seemed to have a different fatal flaw. They were painfully pious or allergic to the cats, or vegetarian and wouldn't serve anything but 'spag-hetti' as father called it. And one seemed to have taken an ominous shine to Leslie – we feared we might get landed with a stepmother before we got him to France.

Then one day we found a lovely Korean girl who wanted to improve her English. Hee-Won had been a Korean Airways Flight Attendant – First Class of course. She mixed Leslie's whisky and water just as he liked it and served it on a little tray with nibbles. She even made those triangles on the end of the loo paper when she changed the roll. The fact that she cooked like a flight attendant, heating food on our best porcelain plates which went all brown and crazed - and turned all Leo's hand-washable jumpers into baby-clothes in the tumble dryer - and according to our daughters – had an endless list of other dismal failings - we loved her, Leslie loved her, the cats loved her. She was perfect.

So we were free to set off for France in search of our dream home! We started at the west side of our imaginary arc, making our first exploratory search into the Loire region where a miniature white stone chateau with a gleaming slate roof, two towers and a garden that sloped down to a river, lured us. With hearts beating in our chests, we caught our first sight of it. We paused, two wheels up on the verge and viewed our future paradise: creamy stone, silvery roofs, a meadow beyond with the tiniest glimpse of shining water.

Me: 'Wow!'.

Him: 'Hmm.'

I gave him a hard look. I was already planting an imaginary avenue of trees running down to the front entrance. At that point a long convoy of trucks full of rubble rumbled past. The agent hurried us on. He spent ages drawing our attention to the finer points of the exterior while I was aching to get inside. At last he turned the key in the front door.

We were met by a strong smell of damp. Of course the place needs airing, it's been locked up for some time, he commented breezily. In the gloom a number of religious statues gazed up to the heavens. I followed their gaze. By the look of it the owners had put more faith in divine intervention than in decent roofers –rain had been seeping through the ceilings for god knows how long. We trailed behind the agent, being treated to a blanket dose of sales-speil, through brown room after brown room, each furnished with a decaying layer of damp and lumpy carpet that felt as if it had dead dogs under it. He threw open a couple of windows, an action poorly timed, as the next convoy of trucks from the neighbouring quarry hove into sight.

Over the following months our exploratory arc took us weekend by weekend through the lesser-known regions of France. Forget desirable Dordogne, Brit-invaded Bordeaux and pricey Provence, we were in search of the real France, authentic and unspoilt. Every few weeks a potential new property lured us across the Channel, convinced that this find would be *the one*. There was the fairytale chateau with its six conical towers, a centuries-old avenue of plane trees and a vast renaissance stone bas-relief set into a wall. As we approached, a peacock strutted arrogantly across our path – I tried to catch Peter's eye - bliss! My enthusiasm started to flag when confronted by acres of rooms, miles of corridors, thirty bedrooms and still counting. It was a mini Versailles and in need of a Sun God's budget to put it to rights.

A smaller, newer, far more sensible chateau, conveniently close to Lyons airport for Peter was our next 'find'. He had become involved in a set of round-the-world seminars, so his time was limited. We flew to Lyons, arriving late on a Saturday afternoon which the agent had grudgingly set aside for us. The photos had suggested a rather spooky place. I was already making noises about being nervous if left alone there. What about burglars or murderers or things that went 'creeeek' in the night? Peter reassured me by pointing out there was a guardian on the premises; if I was alone there with the oldies, this dear dependable vassal would be at hand to fight off these dangers.

Dusk was falling as we wound our way down a long isolated lane that led to his domain. Our first sighting was of a real Bluebeard's castle - all four crenellated towers outlined against an ominous sky. Dogs howled as we passed the guardian's house and a couple of rottweillers threw themselves against the iron grille slavering in fury.

'Handy for security,' Peter commented.

Me: 'Umm.'

The agent was making reassuringly jovial noises about dogs and alarms and the safety of the house in general. I followed him inside with a sinking feeling – nobody could have lived in the place for years – in fact they might even have died and still be there judging by the smell.

'We'd better hurry while the light lasts,' he suggested. 'The electricity has been cut off.'

We followed him groping our way up the dusky staircase. On the upper storey the air was fresher, someone had washed the floors recently and thrown the windows open in an optimistic attempt to dry them. I hugged my coat closer round me trying to look for positives. We hadn't seen the Jardin d'Hiver yet – the prized conservatory, where Leslie was going to read his morning newspaper bathed in warmth and sunlight. The agent led us through to the back of the house where a window looked down on this marvel. A view of broken panes and rusting skeletal ironwork met our gaze.

'Of course it needs a few panes of glass replaced,' he said moving on to view yet more bedrooms.

Somehow I got separated from the others. I had taken a wrong turning and found myself at the dead end of a corridor that led nowhere, trapped in murky darkness. I stood there frozen, fighting down waves of panic. But footsteps were approaching, probably Peter coming back for me. Groping forward to meet him, I met a blood-chilling vision. Wall-eyed and hunched over like Quasimodo on a bad day – I came face to face with the guardian.

As another spring approached we started to feel despondent. We'd planned to be settled in our dream house by the previous summer. But we were wiser and more discerning now. We'd learnt the pretty obvious lesson that the larger the property, the lower the price, since renovation is far more expensive than buying the house itself.

A Maison de Maitre, an ideal much smaller and more appropriate buy, came up. It was near Autun - a rather charming, if remote, town in the wild Morvan region, which has a magnificent cathedral. It was early January, so we wouldn't be blinded to the property's shortcomings by summer sun – this was going to be a sensible purchase. The property was on top of a hill with 360 degree views over rolling countryside. The weather had turned icy. Temperatures sank down to minus 6. Swaddled in coats and scarves we followed the agent round this icy marvel. Visions of the dasha in Dr Zhivago leapt to mind – the interior wasn't actually coated in ice but felt like it.

Peter: 'I've always wanted a view'
Me: 'Umm.'

We cast a discerning eye over heating and plumbing. The roof was sound which was a bonus. And it would have the right amount of accommodation once we added a couple of bathrooms. That night in our hotel room we sketched out a ground plan with the extra bathrooms and a couple of bedrooms moved to the ground floor for the oldies. This meant we could manage a study each and rooms for the girls or guests above. Yes, we could make it work - so next morning we put in an offer and headed for home.

It wasn't exactly love at first sight, it was more a marriage of convenience. As Peter pointed out, it was a sensible buy and we could afford it. And of course it would be so much nicer in the summer. I did a pretty good job of convincing myself that we would be happy there and set to making measured plans and dreaming up ideas for the décor. Then, early one morning, just as we thought everything was settled, we had a call from the agent to say the property had already been sold – under his nose, under our noses – not, we were soon to learn – an uncommon event in France, where any property may be with as many as thirty agents, none of whom communicates with the others.

We sat round the breakfast table feeling desolate. 'I don't think I'm ever going to get to France,' said Leslie. He'd set his heart on the move as much as us. I think he saw himself sitting in some sunny café, with an ever-replenished glass of red wine at his elbow, contentedly reading Figaro for the rest of his life.

Things got worse. A day or so later we got a call from my sister in Australia. Could she come and stay for a while, a month or two? One more person to house. That was it. Plans of battle were drawn up. We would go back and storm the country, search every hill and valley, the house we wanted was out there somewhere - we were going to find it.

We had found an agent we liked – Paolo, he was the person who'd been answering the phone to my stumbling French and then one day he'd said. 'Would you prefer to speak English?' He was half French, half English and when we met him in person standing in front of a village church in a huge Aussie hat with the snow flurrying round him, I fell for his irresistibly wicked smile.

Paolo took us on a vomit-inducing trip through the wildest winding roads of Central France. He showed us, predictably, what we'd come to expect from French agents – all the properties that had been on his books for yonks and were impossible to shift. We ended up one wintry lunchtime with snow threatening in a leaden sky, sitting in a small brasserie, feeling we'd come to the end. We were due to drive back to Paris that afternoon and then on to London. We'd simply run out of properties to view. Warmed by the food and probably by the amount of red wine he'd drunk, Paolo became more voluble. He described the battle he was having with a rogue of a chap who'd set himself up as an agent although he didn't have the official qualifications.

'The cheek of it. He wants to sell his own house and take the commission.'

'Oh,' I said with a yawn, sleepy from the wine. 'What's his house like?'

Paolo reached into his briefcase and drew out a photograph that made my head reel. Had this been planned? Had he taken us on this wild goose chase of totally unsaleable properties to soften us up? Had he left this property till last because he couldn't be sure of getting his cut?

Before us, lay a photograph of a heart-meltingly beautiful house: Sets of tall arched windows looked out over a park. A roof of steely slate led the eye up to a single pyramidal tower. The façade was veiled by wisteria threaded with a single rambling rose that tumbled back down across the double front door.

'La Gozinière,' he said. 'It's 18th Century but in pretty good nick, since it's never been uninhabited. And there are two chambres d'hôtes with bathrooms of the ground floor which might interest you.'

'But it's perfect,' I stammered. 'Why didn't you tell us about it before?'

'I'm not quite sure if it's actually for sale,' he backtracked.

'But can we see it?'

'I could ring the fellow and ask.'

We waited tense minutes while Paolo went out to the parking area where he could get a connection. He seemed to be having some sort of discussion. When he came back he said. 'I've managed to persuade him. But not before four pm.'

'But we're going back to Paris,' said Peter. 'Maybe another time.'

'No,' I said. 'We'll see it today. We can find a hotel for the night and leave tomorrow.'

Peter made some noises of disagreement which I ignored.

'OK. I'll meet you there at four then,' said Paolo.

Of course we didn't wait till four. We drove over and curb-crawled along the lane like burglars casing a joint.

'Oh it's perfect. It's beautiful. I want it,' I said peering through the hedge.

'We haven't seen inside yet,' said Peter.

'I don't care. This is it. This is the house we've been looking for.'

Chapter Three

Six months have passed and I'm actually standing outside the front door of 'La Gozinière' with the key in my hand. The house is ours. Few things compete with this moment on the scale of happiness or achievement. Getting a degree? The birth of a baby? A book published? Not one of them comes even near.

We'd last seen the house on that darkening February afternoon with Paolo. The proprietor had come to the door wiping his hands on an oily rag (we later found he'd spent the last three hours trying to get the worn out central heating boiler to work). Paolo had warned us not to look too interested – the man was a rogue (it takes one to know one). So we followed behind the two of them as po-faced as we could manage. The ground floor still had its parquet intact and as the owner threw open the sets of double doors, one after the other, we found room after room, all with high ceilings and finely proportioned. They still had their original 18th Century features - some were panelled, some had painted over-door frescoes. We paused in the hallway – the original massive oak staircase curving up above us to a beamed ceiling.

I exchanged glances with Peter. Or to be more exact my look of total ecstasy was met by his blank non-commital stare.

Up the staircase we went on into the bedrooms – not too many - only ten-ish - quite reasonable compared with some of the houses we'd seen – a couple of them were locked and the fellow mumbled something about having lost the key. But why worry, we'd need some non-descript rooms for storage, I whispered to Peter. He was still steadfastly 'not-looking-interested', in fact he was so good at it that I was starting to panic. Finally, we were led into the tower - up a creamy stone spiral staircase and into the attic - a vast cathedral space with beams as thick as ship's timbers. The owner thrust a shutter open in one of the dormers to let in some light and as he did so a flurry of snow flew in, creating a dazzling display of white specks in the darkness. I stood transfixed. He was rabbiting on about the size of the park and the brilliance of the view on a clear day. But there could have been a nuclear power station in the neighbouring field as far as I cared. We'd found it - our dream house. I was going to have this house, no matter what, nothing was going to get in my way.

We walked in silence back to the cars. As I climbed into ours I stared in fury at Peter – he still had that maddening non-committal face on.

'If you don't want this house, I'm divorcing you,' I said.

'Shhhh! The bloke's still watching us.'

We overtook Paolo in the lane and arranged to meet him at the nearest bar.

'Put an offer in now, right away,' we said as he carried the drinks to the table.

'But you haven't seen all the rooms yet,' he said.

'Doesn't matter. We want it.'

'You don't want to look too keen.'

'We don't want to lose it either.'

There followed two tense weeks of wrangling. We'd left Paolo in charge of the negotiations and were back in London. God knows what was taking so much time, I literally hit the roof every time the phone rang. But one evening I answered it to hear Paolo's voice with his inimitable chuckle: 'I've got good news for you,' he said.

I burst into tears. The family had gathered round and were watching me in horror.

'No,' I sobbed. 'We've got it! It's ours.'

Leslie had to have several whiskies to recover and we joined him. I don't think any of us slept much that night from sheer excitement. And now here I was. At last I was unlocking the door to our future home.

As luck would have it Peter had to be in the Far East the week we took possession of the house. I'd come with Juliet, my sister, en route back from a painting trip to the South of France. The key had been left with a neighbour – an English neighbour - ominously. I'd primed Juliet not to be too friendly – the last thing I wanted when moving to France was to have an English neighbour constantly on our doorstep inviting us to those inevitable endless boozy expat lunches and evening gins and tonic. And to make things worse, this neighbour was from the *North* of England.

'Hello, I'm Pam,' said the woman who greeted us with an open smile and a warmth to her and a softness to that dreaded Northern accent. She made us coffee, which we drank in the garden with Noel her husband – a big man with a white beard who I noted at the time wasn't in the best of health. I was right about this – sadly, a month or so later – Noel died suddenly in the night.

But that morning he entertained us with a deadpan rendition of hilarious jokes while Pam made proper coffee and served it in tiny porcelain coffee cups. Well, we were the folk from the big house after all. We didn't stay long – by eye-contact I'd reminded my sister that we didn't want to get too pally.

Turning down Pam's kind offer of lunch we made for the house. The key turned in the lock. The entry hall greeted us, as tall and grand and majestic as I remembered it.

The rooms, now empty of the previous owner's dubious taste in furniture looked, if anything, even lovelier than they had before.

'Wow,' said Juliet after I'd shown her round, brimming with pride. 'How are you going to make it liveable in?'

'It is liveable in!'

'Well, don't think I'm staying here in its present state. Come on, there's no hot water, the kitchen's a shambles, everything's covered in dust - and what are you going to do about all these cobwebs?'

'Brush them away! A few telephone calls and I'll get some builders to tackle the rest.'

So we holed up in a local hotel. The hoteliers kindly gave me their old telephone directory and I started on an initial round of calls to roofers and plumbers, carpenters and electricians, persuading them to take a break from the serious business of having their summer holiday and come and give quotes.

Three more months went by and no work was done on the house. We were busy putting our house in Fulham on the market and I was making it look as saleable as possible. The agent's photographer was coming round, I had filled the place with flowers and brushed the cats. The fellow was hardly over the doorstop with his camera when the agent rang and asked if one of his clients could have a sneak preview. The client was a banker and I think he must have just received his bonus because he offered us five per cent over the asking price if we would take it off the market. We accepted his offer on the spot.

Now we had a bonus to spend on La Gozinière. Peter had finished his round of world seminars and could actually take a break. Like a couple of (aged) honey-mooners we drove over to France in a trance of excitement. It was September, the late summer weather was quite glorious. We'd booked rooms in the little local hotel I'd stayed in with my sister. But we found a bed in the barn and a mattress still in its plastic packaging. We decided to shun the hotel and camp in the house. We had a bed and a bath with water that heated up in a noisy and reluctant way - and a camping gaz to cook on. We didn't mind not having chairs or a table or curtains, we ate out in restaurants or picnicked in the garden. It was a heavenly period, we were both in love with the house. We slept in what we called the 'art nouveau' bedroom which had panelling carved eccentrically in a rather rustic version of Gallé. Some years later I met the son of the carpenter responsible for it. His father had been hard pressed apparently to please his client. Curtainless, we slept with the long windows open to the night sky. In the clear Bourbonnais air the stars were as bright as fireworks and when the moon was full it cast shadows across the lawn. Owls hunted in the garden and occasionally small bats fluttered across our faces. For two townees like us, everything had an irresistible charm - the smell of fresh mown grass, the sound of tractors working in the fields at night, even the far too early crowing of cocks.

We walked down the lane and got to know Pam properly. She gave us the names and numbers of other, better, cheaper builders than the ones I'd found in the directory. I rang for more quotes and showed more men, clucking and sucking through their teeth, around the house. What work had been done so far had been done by what they called, disparagingly – 'bricoleurs'. I'd never come across the word for these thieves and rogues. The dictionary provided the answer – DIY enthusiasts. Most of the work they were complaining about had been done by the fellow we bought the house from, the 'rogue' M.Sandrin. We coined a new word for a particularly bad piece of workmanship - a 'Sandrinage'.

Reluctantly, in October, we returned to London, leaving a roofer who gave promises that he would start the following week. Calls back and forth between me and Pam soon established that this was pure fiction, the workers never turned up. By November it was clear that someone would have to live in the house to ensure any work was done. Peter was up to his eyes in important money-earning consultancy jobs so the task fell to me.

I drove South with the car weighed down with bedding and kitchen ware, spades and gumboots, spending a night in Paris with Claudia. Arriving in the evening at La Gozinière was magical. I slowed the car and left it in the avenue, approaching the house on foot so as to savour the stillness of the garden, the freshness of the evening.

Inside all was still. I walked from room to room, my footsteps echoing on the parquet. Unfurnished, as it was, the house seemed to have slipped back in time. I might well have been back in the 18th Century. The slanting evening sun gave the place a soft Vermeer-like quality. I felt as if, at any moment, I might come across one of its former residents, scratching with a quill at a ledger or practising her scales on a clavicord. Room opened into room in a way that made me wonder if anyone had ever had any privacy. Like most 18th Century houses, the builders hadn't bothered with corridors. What was the point? Maids and servants would have been in and out all the time with firewood or hot water. They'd dress you and wash you (occasionally). Bed curtains were about all you'd have by way of modesty.

The art nouveau bedroom and the neighbouring one had a small anteroom between them. A servant's room most probably. I paused here thinking this was just the sort of room that Count Almaviva might have given Figaro and Susanna in The Marriage of Figaro. Next door to his room so that Susanna could be 'on tap' so to speak when the fancy took him. It was a small-ish room – Figaro would have to measure carefully to find the place to position the bed.

Perhaps this was when the idea took hold in my subconscious. La Goziniere was built in 1758 – the date was inscribed in the lintel over the central dormer – a time of relative peace and prosperity, thirty-five or so years before the Revolution. It was around this time that Beaumarchais wrote the play on which Mozart's opera was based.

I stood their fantasising. It was a totally mad idea really – that once the house was restored to life and up and running – we'd put on a performance of 'The Marriage of Figaro' to celebrate. It was mad considering the dilapidated state of the place. And an impossibly extravagant idea too, operas are costly affairs. But I think that was the moment the seed was sown.

All through the agonies and ecstasies of the renovation, which took two years in all, rather than our hopelessly optimistic estimate of four months - the idea lurked at the back of my mind, surfacing sometimes in dreams or in idle moments in the bath, building castles in the air. But as we'd discovered with finding the house, fantasies have a way of coming true.

Chapter Four

'You know what I'd really like?' It was now or never, somehow I had to get the rest of the family to agree to my hair-brained idea.

It's December and we're all sitting round the kitchen table discussing how we're going to mark the official house warming - or as the French say to: 'Pendre la cremaillère' meaning literally to hang up the funny-iron-thingee-you-suspend-cooking-pots-on in the fireplace. It's planned for August – our new potential date for when the building work will definitively be finished.

Yes, we now have a kitchen table – and a kitchen – two years have passed and the house, at last, is pretty well up and running. Sadly Leslie hasn't made it, he had a fall and broke a hip and died just before our move. But my mother Marjorie has – she's one of the party round the table giving her opinion.

'No, what would you like?' asked Peter.

'I'd like to have a performance of the Marriage of Figaro in the house.'

Response: general amusement and scorn from all corners of the table.

'No, I'm being serious. We'll invite all the people who've ever lived here. We could dress up!'

'In 18th Century costume?' More derision.

'My birthday's in August,' says Claudia. 'Why don't we just give a party? I know a guy at the Bains-Douches – the D.J. – he'd probably bring all the equipment. I've got loads of friends in Paris who'd come.'

At the mention of the Bains-Douches (ex-public baths, currently a stylish Parisian night spot) visions of carloads of young Parisians leapt to mind - all smoking as if their life depended on it, lounging on our new beds, drinking our cellar dry and spilling red wine on our pristine wallcoverings, snorting coke in the shrubbery and generally being impossibly cool and laid-back and too beautiful to do anything but pose throughout the house. The last lot Claudia brought home we christened the Gucci Loafers.

'Think of the noise,' said Peter.

Claudia leant back in her chair and yawned. 'The cows won't mind. Who's to care round here anyway?'

'We are,' said Peter and I in unison.

'Where would you get the costumes anyway?' asked Claudia.

'We could make them,' suggested Pam. (Yes, I'd given in. Northern on not, Pam's incredible energy, cleverness, kindness and boundless source of fun had ground me down. She was a friend, a sister, a part of the family who everyone loved – even Marjorie).

'But is it such a mad idea?' I countered

'Where on earth would you find an opera company willing to come out to some remote region of France?' said Peter in a tone which should have stopped the subject dead.

'I could ask Jimmy's girlfriend,' says Claudia getting up from the table and re-filling her glass with wine. 'She works for some sort of music school.'

Me: 'What's it called?'

Claudia; 'Dunno, it's in London. Royal Something.'

'Royal Academy of Music?'

'That's it.'

'Try her. Ring her then.'

A few weeks later I had a call from Jimmy.

'I hear you want to put on an opera in your house.'

I gripped the receiver more firmly. 'Yes, that's right. Yes we do.'

'Well, I don't think we can manage an opera. But we might be able to do something choral.'

'Oh?'

'My girlfriend Helen and I are coming to France next month. We're driving round looking for locations for a choral workshop. We need pretty big houses, Claudia said yours might be suitable.'

'We need something to be performed in August.'

'That would fit. The workshops have to be in the college holidays.'

'Well, come then, and take a look. We'd be only too happy to put you up.'

It was February. A cold wet grey February. We were into the shortest days of the year. A misty stillness enveloped the house, nothing actually moved apart from the buzzards wheeling overhead hoping to spot a potential meal moving in the grass. We were missing the lights and animation of London. At this time of year a couple of young guests would be a bonus.

'What day are they coming,' asked Peter.

'Next Thursday. Some time in the evening.'

'Oh not Thursday. We've promised to take Marjorie out to that sauerkraut dinner.'

'They can come too.'

'What if they don't like sauerkraut?'

'Tough.'

'What if they don't get here in time?'

'We can leave a note. They can join us there.'

'Are you sure you know what you're doing?'

'It's only two young people for a night.'

The sauerkraut dinner was in a neighbouring village. As anticipated, Jimmy and Helen didn't turn up on time. It was a gloomy evening with an icy mist rapidly turning to thick fog. The fog was no doubt responsible for their delay. Pam, Peter and I bundled Marjorie – never one to be late for a meal (or a drink) into the car and set off leaving a note with a map stuck to the front door.

The village hall turned out to be the venue for the dinner. Not quite what I'd expected. Trestle tables with shiny oil-cloths and plastic chairs had been set out under violently bright strip-lighting. There was no sign of any sauerkraut but a promising farty odour was emanating from the kitchens. We exchanged glances, should we back out now? But we had six people to feed and nothing ready at home. We'd have to make the best of it and hope that Jimmy and Helen weren't too grand. So we sat Marjorie down and waited.

'I could do with a drink,' said Marjorie, voicing all our thoughts.

I ventured towards the kitchen and leant in. Four aproned bottoms were turned, concentrating on something grey-green in huge metal oven trays.

'Excuse me. I have a ninety-two year old lady outside who is rather thirsty,' I said.

A woman with enormous red arms reared up from the group. 'J'arrive!' she announced – which is French for 'in-my-own-good-time'.

Another half hour went by. Marjorie was starting to get tetchy. Pam said: 'I've had enough of this,' rose from her chair, marched into the kitchen and returned with a five litre jug of Kir and a roll of plastic glasses.

The kir improved Marjorie's mood somewhat. More people started to turn up, lingering with embarrassment in the doorway then shuffling in, in a variety of work boots and freshly pressed leisurewear. These were country people in their own environment. They sidled past us with a polite 'Bonsoir' and a suspicious look. What were we doing at their village soirée? We nodded and raised our glasses to them. After an hour of nothing but kir, I started to worry about the logistics of getting Marjorie back in the car. And my head was starting to swim. We were all in need of solid food to sop up the kir. Emboldened by my inebriated state I made another foray into the kitchen.

'We have a ninety-two year old outside and she's very hungry.' In fact, the ninety two year old was quite happily toasting everyone around the room – I was the one who was hungry.

This statement seemed to provoke an avalanche of sauerkraut. Plates piled with mountains of food were placed before us. More wine was produced and by the general rise in the volume of talk you could tell the party had begun.

But still no Jimmy and Helen. I secured two platefuls for them and covered them with kitchen foil. Music had started up in the adjoining room - an out-of tune squeeze-box and someone trying to murder a violin. I was having deep misgivings about inviting our Royal Academy friends – no doubt they'd be quiet serious types who scorned anything less than Baroque.

People were rising from their tables to dance. A fellow grabbed Pam and whisked her into the next room. Men were stamping their feet and calling for more wine, a baby had started crying, the noise level was deafening. Then just as I thought we should get up and make a move for home, the door was flung open. Accompanied by a puff of freezing fog a couple of young strangers entered the room. Jimmy and Helen.

Shouting over the hub-bub, I tried to apologise for the set-up finding them knives and forks and more plastic glasses and settling them down. Marjorie by now was well ready for bed, so Peter and I left Pam in charge of the Londoners and made a hasty exit.

Sometime around three in the morning I heard a car sweep to a halt on the gravel outside. I turned over thinking I was imagining things – they must have been back ages ago.

At breakfast we learned from Pam how the evening had progressed after we'd left. The dancing had got wilder and wilder (Pam had actually got whirled around by some stranger and snogged). Jimmy and Helen had been in the thick of it. It had ended with the pair of them up on a table supporting each other while Helen belted out Edith Piaf songs to massive applause. We'd made our mark. In fact, we were famous in the area.

Jimmy came down the next morning looking very sorry for himself. I dosed him on Nurofen and coffee and showed him round the house. He looked more and more glum as we went round.

'You don't like the house?' I asked.

'I love the house. It's just that I wouldn't want to let one of our choir-courses loose in it. You know things can get a bit out of hand. We were in a chateau last year and a huge gilt mirror got smashed.'

Remembering the account of the night before I said: 'Oh – I see.'

Later that day we watched Jimmy and Helen drive off in search of a more suitable venue for their choir course. In my mind visions receded of the garden decked with 18th Century costumed figures, the chords of Mozart ringing out in the warmth of the evening, the final arias rising from the darkness of the box walk. Well, we'd tried. It had been a lovely idea. We'd just have to give a nice dinner for our house-warming. Pity, but still.

Chapter Five

A couple of months later, when I'd resigned myself to the fact that my opera evening was never going to take place, the phone rang.

'Hello. You don't know me. My name's Jane, Jane Mabbitt. I hear from Jimmy that you want to give an opera in your house.'

'Yes,' I said warily, I'd been here before. 'Yes, we do.'

'Well, I don't know how we'd work this, but we're a troupe of young singers. We belong to Bedfordshire Youth Opera. We're mostly students but very good. We've put together an opera using arias from Mozart..'

'Mozart?' Could I be hearing this?

'Yes, it's a modern story but all the music's Mozart. We're taking it round schools.'

'But could you do it here, in France, in August?'

'Quite possibly. If we could find a way to get everyone out there.'

I took her name and details and fighting back mounting excitement went to find Peter. He was up on his vegetable patch waging his on-going battle against Colorado beetle.

'I've had a call from a girl who says she can do an opera for us.'

'You're not still going on about Figaro?' he said grinding a gumboot on to an advancing Colorado legion.

'No, not actually Figaro. They've got an opera all rehearsed and ready and everything – but it is Mozart. And she thinks they could do it in August.'

He exterminated another dozen beetles and looked up.

'But we're nowhere near ready for a house-warming.'

It was true, with the inevitable delays and set-backs that occur in any building project, our optimistic finishing date had been pushed forward once more.

'But don't you see. This is an opportunity that may never come up again. If we say 'no' - that will be it.'

'They could always do it next year.'

I stood my ground. 'No you have to grasp these things when they happen. They'll probably give up on us if we put them off now.'

'But the courtyard isn't even paved yet.' It was true, road-builders with a bulldozer were due to come and break up the hideous old cement terrace. Once this was gone we were going to lay a new stone terrace which was to serve as our stage. But the road builders cancelled twice already.

'But they're bound to come before August. We'll have the courtyard ready by then.'

'Give me time to think about it.'

I went back to the kitchen steaming. Think about it! This offer was too good to be missed.

I waited diplomatically until evening, when Peter had had his meal and evening glass or two of wine, before bringing the subject up again.

'So have you thought about it?' I asked tentatively.

'I've been trying to work out how we could get them here,' he said.

I could have thrown my arms around his neck and kissed him but the battle wasn't won yet. I needed to sound diplomatically doubtful myself.

'But they may not be any good. Youth Opera, I mean, it could be embarrassingly bad.'

'No-one's going to be embarrassed. Not if we have a dinner interval and give them a really good meal. The French will put up with anything if you feed them properly.'

'We'll make a big effort. We could give them champagne.' I agreed.

'But we've still got to get them here.'

'There must be a way. A group Eurostar ticket. A mini-bus. Easyjet, I don't know. How does anyone get anywhere?'

'And we'll need an audience. You can't perform an opera to a handful of people.'

'How many were you thinking of inviting?'

'I've been making a list.'

I gave him a hug - perhaps our marriage had a future after all.

The next day I got on to Jane. 'We've been talking it over. We think it could work. But we've got a load of questions.'

Over several phone sessions we worked through the logistics. What about an orchestra? No problem, they were using a piano score and they could bring their own portable electric piano. How could they travel with a piano? They could borrow the college mini-bus as long as we paid for the ferry, petrol and tolls. Would they need paying? Not if we covered all their expenses, put them up and fed them. It would be a working holiday, they'd do the performance for us as a thank you. What about costumes and props? They had them already, no costumes were needed as their opera was set in the present day.

We were on! We had our opera. I flew in to a whirlwind of preparations. We had nine bedrooms, four of which were still in need of decoration. We occupied one, Marjorie another. My sister had been invited over from Australia and our two daughters and boyfriends would need to be put up. That was five bedrooms gone – leaving four free and eight performers to accommodate. They'd have to double up and we'd make a dormitory for the boys. We'd need more beds and bedding, blinds and curtains and towels…

Trips were made into the neighbouring towns of Moulins and Montluçon. Pam had introduced me to Emmaüs - the amazing French charity warehouses which are run in aid of the homeless. She's one of their best customers. She's worried about money now she's a widow and has decided to convert her attic into rooms to let as Chambres d'Hôtes (the French for B&B). We join forces on shopping trips, vying over iron beds which are going for a pittance and source mattresses from the bargain store Noz – an Aladdin's cave of bankrupt stock, seconds and fraudulent fire damage where everything is brand new and just that little bit second-rate. We load up her clapped-out Renault Espace and come home with mountains of duvets and sacks of towels. I snap up a nesting stack of enormous stainless steel saucepans. We already have a semi-professional six-burner cooker but everything else needed for catering on this scale has to be thought of.

By now it was May and a steady rain had set in. We hadn't bargained on this – wasn't this France? Wasn't this the land of endless sunfilled holidays? The driveway and courtyard had turned into a potholed morass. The plumber, who was busy re-directing the pipes from the septic tank to comply with the new European directives, seemed to be in league with the weather. Trenches kept appearing in unlikely places and the trip to the car was a precarious journey across wobbling planks. The house became an island surrounded by what looked like one of the wetter days in the battle of the Somme. No-one could venture outside without gumboots. And then just when we thought it couldn't get any worse, the road builders arrived churning their way up the drive with their bulldozer and mechanical diggers.

The cats watched in horror from the kitchen window as what looked like an enormous dinosaur bashed and reared and lifted vast slabs of concrete into the air and slammed them down into a skip. It took a day to destroy the old terrace and then their foreman slapped a bill into my hand and drove off leaving us with a desolate moonscape of a courtyard.

'It'll be fine when it's paved,' said Peter as we gazed out at it glumly.

We'd decided to lash out on the terrace, we'd ordered real stone – lovely creamy Loire stone, the house deserved nothing less. We'd found a stone supplier in Chateauneuf-sur-Cher. They'd come and measured and they'd promised to prepare all the edging stones with expensive rounded borders. I'd asked, to their surprise, for the very worst stone they had, the more fissures and marks the better – we wanted it to blend with the shabby aged texture of the house.

I rang the stone merchants with the good news. We were ready for them. Oh, but they couldn't possibly deliver it right away. Oh no Madame, they still had the cutting and finishing to do. June was already booked up. There were all the public holidays to take into account and the 'ponts' which meant in effect they were working a three-day week. And then of course July and August were holiday months – the office would be shut down. They'd book as in for September – we'd be their very first job of the new season. I pleaded and cajoled but to no avail. We'd held them up because the road builders had held us up and now we were stuck in a queue of other equally demanding clients.

I put the phone down. 'So no courtyard,' I told Peter.

'We'll have to cancel the opera. Thank god we haven't sent out the invitations yet.'

'No, we can't. They've booked the ferry and everything. We can't disappoint them now.'

'We can't disappoint you.'

'Yes, well there's that too.'

I stared out of the window. One of the cats was taking advantage of the newly cleared space and digging a hole. He turned round to face us and sat over it doing an arrogant pee in what would have been the centre of our stage.

'There's always the attic,' I said. This great cathedral space had suddenly taken on a new significance.

'It's filthy and full of rubbish. That rogue we bought the place from should have cleared it. There's woodworm in the boards. I'm not even sure the floor will hold.'

'It's got to be cleared anyway and we should be doing something about the woodworm.'

'It'll be too hot in August.'

'We can open the dormers and put in more veluxes.'

Pam arrived at the back door with a basket of cherries from her tree. They were black and at the ultimate point of ripeness.

'What's up?'

'They can't do the courtyard till September. Peter thinks we should cancel the opera. But I don't see why we can't use the attic.'

'We'd never have it ready in time,' said Peter.

'Who says?' said Pam giving him a handful of cherries. I could sense her mentally rolling up her sleeves.

'Let's sleep on it. We don't have to make a decision right away,' I suggested.

The following morning Peter had to leave for a meeting in Switzerland. I drove him to Moulins to take the train to Paris and then on by air to Geneva. We still hadn't made a decision. He agreed reluctantly to leave it till he came back. I drove back to Gozinière feeling really miserable. A break in Switzerland, in that artificial world of suits and board rooms, smart lunches and immaculate hotels, would make Peter even more reluctant to take on the role of the man-of-all-tasks for a do-it-yourself opera.

Approaching the house I noticed one of the attic dormers was open. There was a messy pile of cardboard boxes on the driveway below and, as I watched, a load more rubbish flew out through the dormer and slammed to the ground in a pile of dust to join the pile. I steamed up the spiral stone staircase to find Pam, covered in dust and cobwebs, working like a galley-slave hauling things across the floor and hurling them out of the dormer.

'You shouldn't be doing this. Shouldn't you have a mask on or something?'

'Stop fussing and get changed and help,' was her only reply. 'We've got to get this lot cleared before Peter gets back.'

'We'll never get all this moved by Wednesday.'

'Rubbish.'

'Exactly!'

'We can work all night if necessary.'

'You're impossible.'

'Do you want to do this opera or don't you?'

That was typical of Pam. She'd been there since the very first day backing me up, urging me on, telling me that nothing was impossible. She'd found me at the very dawn of the renovation, sitting despondently at the table in the little breakfast room, practically in tears wondering where to start.

'What's up,' she'd asked. She'd just lost a husband, she should have been the one weeping into her tea.

'This room's so ghastly. Look at it. I don't know where to begin,' I muttered. The walls were covered in the most hideous mustard hessian.

'Make yourself useful. Go to the village and get us some food and buy us some wine,' she said.

'OK.'

I got back half an hour later to find she'd stripped the whole room. We had to spend our first Christmas with naked walls of exposed rubble but they were a lot nicer than the mustard hessian. We festooned them with garlands made out of yew branches and fir cones. The effect was fantastic by candle-light.

Peter got back from Switzerland to find the attic cleared, cobweb-free and swept. We'd ordered a load of floorboards to replace the worm-eaten ones. Pam and I were busy treating them with woodworm killer and Alain our odd-job man was standing by to fit them. We led Peter up the winding stone stairway to the attic and threw open the door 'Dah-dah!'

He let out a low whistle. 'Who did this?'

'Well, Pam mainly. I helped.'

'It's fantastic.'

'It can work, can't it?'

He looked up at the beams. 'We can fix stage lighting up on those.'

We were back on!

Emails had been buzzing back and forth from England. We had a cast list and synopsis. Peter got down to designing the invitations and programmes. He gave Corinne, his French teacher, the job of translating the singers' synopsis into French - their opera was to be performed in English and since the majority of the audience was to be French they would need to have the basics of the story in their own language. Pam and I settled down to the practical side of things.

We bought eight heavy duty reflector lights from a DIY outlet. All these had to be rewired with longer flexes - my job - I'm quite handy with a screwdriver. The electricians, who were still at work in the house, were briefed on adding sockets around the attic walls.

We needed chairs and tables for the supper and a hundred or so more for the performance itself. Yes, the guest list had crept up to a hundred – friends from England wanted to come. Claudia and Leo had already asked their young friends and I had a load of people I wanted to ask because they had been helping me with my research into the history of the house – more of that later.

There are a few things in France that compensate for the shortcomings of the French – like their total lack of customer-service for instance. True to their Liberté, Egalité et Fraternité - as a citizen of a

French village, one has rights – one of these amazingly is to be able to borrow all the Mairie's tables and chairs (provided they're not needed officially) absolutely free. This was the Allier - nothing remotely official was likely to be done in August. So twenty-two tables and two hundred folding chairs were put down in our name to be picked up on the Friday before the opera.

Pam and I now set our minds to that vital dinner that would make up for any shortfall on the musical side. I'd been making enquiries about hiring: tablecloths, china, glasses, knives and forks – if I was going to make a decent dinner, it wasn't going to be eaten off paper plates. 'But Madame – *August.*' All the hire shops are closed for the summer holidays came the shocked reply – fancy trying to entertain in August! One should be at the seaside or in the mountains.

Our only alternative was to buy stuff. We scoured the local brocantes (a rather grand French name for boot sales). Local white china from Limoges must have been the mainstay of many a Bourbonnais bridal list for the past century or so. The remnants of such family services, a little chipped and seldom with its gold rim totally intact, turned up in toppling piles which we bought for a song. Knives and forks were purchased in bunches. Glasses come cheap these days in cellophane-wrapped stacks from the supermarket. We made weekly visits to Emmaüs buying up vast white linen sheets embroidered for the brides of yesteryear with the happy couple's initials. Hopefully some of Emmaüs' homeless got proper modern bed sheets to compensate. It took a month or so to amass enough stock for ten tables. Serving dishes were in shorter supply, so I started to collect the lovely Limoges porcelain tureens. Second-hand, you could either find the tureen or the lid – never the two together. But with patience and a keen eye – tureens and lids were being reunited in the cool depths of our pantry.

Like a miser counting his money I laid out all our purchases on the dining room table and counted and recounted to make sure we had all we needed. Marjorie shuffling past with her walking frame, took one look at the table and muttered darkly about the madness of the whole endeavour.

The opera was timed for the tenth of August. The cast, complete with director, pianist and producer were due to arrive three days earlier in order to rehearse and reblock the opera in the new setting. The opera itself titled 'La Voce di Perdono' or The Voice of Forgiveness (with apologies to Mozart) was the brain child of the Director - Fred Broom. I was coming to the conclusion that this Fred was a bit of a genius. Under his guidance the cast had written the opera themselves, re-scripting the arias, adapting the score and adding link dialogue. It was a massive task, not to mention the slog of cutting and pasting, sno-paking, photocopying and binding the fifteen cast scores they needed. A copy of the score was sent to us ahead of time. It looked fun. We just prayed that their young voices were up to it.

With a month still to go, we were having lunch out on the lawn, sunning ourselves and discussing the final arrangements for the all-important dinner menu for the big night. Pam and I had decided on a buffet so that people could serve themselves, thus eliminating the need for waiters. The elements of this buffet were still up for discussion.

Pam: How about Coronation Chicken, everyone likes that?

Me: Hasn't it got curry powder in it?

Peter: You can't give the French curry, they don't understand it.

Marjorie: So indigestible.

Me: How about cold beef? We could get the butcher to cook it and slice it.

Peter: Too dull.

Marjorie: Might be tough.

Pam: What about sushi?

Peter: You can't have raw fish in this heat, you'll poison everyone.

Marjorie: What's sushi?

Pam: OK, it's got to be cold salmon then.

Me: For a hundred guests plus the singers! You'll need ten fish kettles.

Pam: Nonsense, you can cook it in newspaper.

Marjorie: whose caught the tail end of the sentence (hopeful). Fish and chips?

Pam: No you wrap the raw fish in a sheet of wet newspaper and put it in the oven. When the newspaper's dry you peel it off and the skin comes off with it. Fillet it and Robert est ton oncle.

    Peter (aside): If it's salmon, it'll have to be the Financial Times.
    We all ignore him.
    Me: Whose going to cook ten salmon?
    Pam: Me.
    Honestly?
    Nothing simpler.
    Marjorie: What about bones?
    Peter: I'll do the salad. Straight from the plot.
    Me (relieved): I guess all that leaves for me is to boil the new potatoes.

So it was all settled. Orders were put in for the food. I double checked with the Mairie for the tables and chairs. Peter mowed the lawns with English precision making nice straight stripes down it and M. Aubertin (or M. Aubergine as Marjorie called him) our adorable and devoted gardener, pruned the hedges to within an inch of their lives. The sun was shining and everything was progressing without a hitch until August 1st. Early that morning the phone rang.

    'We seem to have a bit of a problem.' It was Jane.
    My heart sank. The acceptances were arriving by the day.
    'We can't get the mini-bus.'
    It was an insurance problem apparently. Nobody had thought until the last moment about getting a Green Card for the bus. And they'd discovered that Cross-channel insurance is ridiculously expensive. While one is perfectly able to drive practically anywhere on your normal insurance in mainland Europe, the EEC seems to stop dead when it reaches water. The price of bringing a bus across the Channel with young drivers was astronomical.

    Peter started looking into trains and flights. Eurostar, in spite of them being a party and a young party at that - proved really pricey at such short notice. At last he found some flights to Charles de Gaulle. Once in Paris they could then pick up a couple of hire cars and drive down to us – there were just enough seats left – he booked them – phew!

We emailed Jane with the good news and went up to bed and had a decent night's sleep for once. The next day she rang again.

'It's really brilliant that Peter got the flights. The only thing is, if we fly we can't bring the electric piano.'

'Oh that shouldn't be a problem,' I said breezily. 'We'll hire one here. Bit risky bringing a piano all this way, anyway.'

Should you ever consider trying to hire a piano in France in August – don't. I rang round a circle of cities that stretched practically up to Paris. All the musical hire shops were closed for the month. There had to be another solution. It didn't have to be an electric piano of course, Pam had a perfectly serviceable upright to lend us but how do you get a piano up the narrow spiral staircase of an 18th Century tower? There was however a doorway at the top of the tower overlooking the courtyard. A doorway that led scarily to nowhere but a forty metre drop. I snatched up a tape measure and ran up the staircase and measured it. We could just get Pam's piano through the doorway but it would take a crane to lift it up there. I rang the local roofer. M. Vrillac had what he called a Manuscopic – a crane thingee with a cage at the top. He drove over to take a look. Then we went down to Pam's to check out the piano. He lifted a corner of it, wincing expressively at the weight. He shook his head. 'No,' he said. 'He couldn't risk it.' The piano was too heavy.

Peter was away finishing off a last bit of work in Switzerland before the summer recess. I was alone and helpless. My house was about to be invaded by eight singers who were total strangers. A hundred or so guests had accepted our kind invitation for a musical evening with a dinner. Except there wasn't going to be any music unless the singers could sing unaccompanied. What was I going to do? Ring them all up and cancel?

With an amazing stroke of serendipity the doorbell rang at that point. I went and opened it. I found Christian, our local vet and new-found friend, standing outside holding a small box.

'A present for you,' he said.

'Come in. I'll make you a coffee. I need cheering up.'

I went and put the coffee on.

'Aren't you going to open your present?'

'I'm not really interested unless there's a piano inside,' I said. 'A piano that could grow to a reasonable size.'

'It's not a piano – something much nicer.'

I opened the box and nearly dropped it. Inside was a small brown salamander. I'm not keen on reptiles at the best of times and this wasn't one of my better days.

'It's a mate for your fellow in the cellar,' he said. 'We couldn't leave the poor chap down there all alone.' It was true, we had a salamander in the cellar – a slow-moving lizard that was a rather alarming black and yellow colour that made me jump every time I went down there. I'd told Christian about him and he'd warned me to take care, yellow and black were warning signs, salamanders were able to spit venom. But he'd have to spit a pretty long way to affect me. I steered well clear of him.

'How do we know if it's male or female?' I asked.

'We don't. But how do we know what yours is? We'll find out no doubt all in good time.'

We took the new brown salamander down to meet his/her future mate. Judging by the black and yellow one's reaction, this would be no whirlwind romance.

'So what did you mean about the piano?' asked Christian when we were back drinking our coffee. I told him the sorry tale about the minibus and the hire shops and Pam's upright and the roofer.

'But I've got a piano,' he said. 'An electric one, Yamaha. I bought it for my daughter a few years ago but she's hardly played it. You can borrow it, no worries.'

I stared at him in disbelief: 'Serendipity!' I breathed.

'What is zat?'

'You coming here today with the salamander! Oh, Christian you've saved my life!'

I would have thrown my arms around his neck, but knowing French men this could have been misinterpreted, so I made him a second coffee instead.

Chapter Six

Nothing could go wrong now. Well, it could. But it didn't. At least not yet. We woke early on the morning the singers were due to arrive. Their beds were all made with a towel neatly folded on each. The fridge and pantry were full of food, the cellar full of wine. Christian's piano was already up in the attic with a dust sheet draped over it. The sun was already streaming in through the window. It was going to be a perfect day.

That morning we went about the house making final arrangements. Peter was printing out parking signs and making table plans and fielding phone calls from various people who'd left it to the last moment to accept our invitation – mainly Claudia's young Parisians.

The singers were due to touch down at three, which meant they could pick up the hire cars and drive down in time for a civilised pre-dinner drink, a nice relaxed time to get to know each other. I'd planned a treat supper for them, or as much of a treat as my mass-catering skills could tackle. I'd had a big Bouef Bourguignon in a slow oven for hours with lots of wine in it and a summer pudding to follow made with fruit from the garden.

At about three-thirty the phone rang.

'If that's another of Claudia's lot wanting to bring a friend tell them 'No',' said Peter.

But it wasn't, it was Fred. 'We're all here all right. I mean not quite all, Jane missed the plane. But we've got a bit of a problem with the hire cars.'

'What sort of a problem? I'm paying, I've given them my banker's details,' said Peter.

'They won't release them to us unless we can produce a credit card.'

'Well, let them have yours. I'll settle up with you later.'

'The thing is – none of us has a credit card.'

'What? There are eight, no seven, of you. Surely one of you must.'

'No. I've asked everyone.'

'Let me talk to the hire guy,' I said taking the phone from Peter.

I brought out my best and most persuasive French, but argue as I might, he was adamant. It was more than his job was worth to release a car without having a credit card swiped through his blasted machine. I told Fred I'd ring him back - we'd think of something.

We rang our bank but since it was a Monday, they were closed. Their answerphone message kept spewing out choices of services, none of which applied to us. We sat staring disconsolately at each other.

'I suppose I could drive to Paris,' suggested Peter.

'That'll take four hours. That's ridiculous,' I said.

'But there's no other option.'

'I'll ring Claudia,' I said.

'How can she help? She doesn't have a credit card.'

(Not likely. Claudia and a credit card would be a fine recipe for disaster). But I rang her anyway.

She was at work. I explained the problem.

'I suppose I could ring Charles,' she said.

'Who's Charles? Does he have a credit card?'

'I should hope so. He practically owns a bank.'

'Charles who?'

'Charles Simon-Thomas. You must remember him. He came to London.'

I searched my memory, flicking through the mental card index of her exes and Charles ... yes Charles Simon-Something did ring a bell.

'He'll get one of his banking people to fix it. Tell the guy if they don't let them have the cars they'll bankrupt their company or something. Leave it with me.'

I rang Fred back to say we were working on a solution. I felt sorry for this Charles. I did remember him, one of Claudia's more amenable conquests – and he had been brought to London – separate bedrooms as I recollect.

Fred rang back jubilantly an hour or so later. They'd got the cars, they were on the road. I didn't hear the whole story till some time later. Apparently, on receiving Claudia's message, this poor unfortunate Charles had walked out of a meeting, taken a taxi to Charles de Gaulle, dazzled all the singers in his dark suit and shiny black shoes, produced a Gold Card from his immaculate wallet and released the cars. The power of woman!

Peter and I waited till nine-thirty with the Bouef Bourguignon getting perceptively drier. We'd packed Marjorie off to bed ages ago. My sister, still jet-lagged from her flight from Australia was well off in the land of nod. Even Pam who'd come over to greet them and had been doing sterling work trying to reduce the European wine lake, went of unsteadily back to her home. By ten I turned off the oven and we ate our dinner.

'Do you think they're lost?'

'Probably.'

At eleven-thirty we decided to go to bed. We'd get some rest at least. At about one in the morning I was woken by the sound of cars crunching over the gravel. I shook Peter awake and we hurried downstairs in our dressing gowns.

'Oh my god, I'm so sorry. We got lost. Are we late?' said a voice. 'It's wonderful to be here. This house is awesome! How do you do. I'm Roland.' I felt suddenly relieved. The fellow looked totally unfazed after their ordeal. The others huddled in after him and stood in a sheepish group by the door.

'I'm Fred,' said a roly-poly Billy Bunter of a person breaking out of the group and coming forward to shake us by the hand. For some reason I'd been expecting a skinny academic, a kind of young Jonathon Miller with a touch of Simon Rattle about him. His glasses were about the only thing they had in common.

He introduced the cast in turn. Donna, a soprano, who was either so tired or so shy she couldn't look up from her feet.

'Would it be all right to call my parents to say we've arrived safely?' she asked in a whisper of a voice. I just prayed she could sing louder.

'Of course,' I showed her to the phone. 'Won't it be a bit late for them?' They were an hour ahead in England. 'No, they said they'd wait up.'

I discovered later, Donna was only sixteen, and this was the first time she'd been outside the UK. Dan Smith, the tenor followed, firm handshake nice straight teeth. Next came a boy called Max, the baritone and then Kitty, another soprano with a gorgeous smile - strong handshake for a girl.

Roland, the pianist, was already deep in conversation with Peter. He was a bit older than the others I noticed. It was reassuring to know we had someone a bit more mature with all these youngsters.

'Would anyone like anything to eat? Or maybe you ate on the way?'

Foolish question. Few people are hungrier than opera singers – troops maybe, prisoners on parole?

'Food first and show you to your rooms after?'

No contest. Peter opened bottles of red while I doled out what I considered massive portions of Bourguignon and mash. Only Donna demurred and sat cradling a cup of cocoa.

As the bottles of wine were passed around the table I started to revise my opinion - sheepish NOT – they were more like a pack of ravening wolves. Second helpings - and even a third for Kitty – disappeared. My mammoth Le Creuset cooking pot was scraped clean. The Summer Pudding met a similar fate.

And then 'Up the wooden stair to Bedfordshire.' Sorry couldn't resist that one.

Peter and I went to bed for the second time that night.

'They seem to enjoy their food,' he commented.

Me: And wine!

'Might have to bump up the shopping list somewhat.'

'Double it.'

'What are you planning for breakfast?'

'Not enough.'

We could hear bumping of luggage on the stairs, footsteps, laughter and shushing and then suddenly, miraculously, silence.

Gozinière lay under a starry sky, the dawn just lightening the rim of the horizon. I felt an incredible sense of fulfilment. The house was full. It was doing its job.

Chapter Seven

The following morning they made a predictably late start. Roland was the first to come down.

'Can I do anything to help?'

Peter had been to the Boulangerie and brought back a couple of the huge loaves we'd specially ordered. I'd put out slabs of local butter and a selection of my home-made jams plus a load of yogurts in those little glass pots that look like miniature milk churns. A couple of saucepans of water were on the boil in addition to the kettle ready for coffee and tea. Hopefully French breakfast would be enough for them.

They came down in dribs and drabs, variously hung over or sleepy, I'd forgotten how difficult young people find mornings. Fred was the last to arrive. He took a cup of coffee and went outside with it to smoke.

'I didn't think singers smoked,' I whispered to Peter, casting a disapproving eye through the window. Wrong. The majority of this group were chain-smokers. I soon gave up putting out ashtrays and provided a planter full of sand instead.

Once Fred had finished his fag he wanted to do a recce of the opera's location. I led them up to the attic. Fred was unimpressed.

'But I thought you did the operas anywhere - in schools and things.'

But he'd had a look round the house the night before. Somehow he'd got it into his head that he could act the scenes out in various rooms in the house moving the audience round with the action.

'But half the time, you'd have the singers inside and audience outside, craning in through the windows.'

He grinned persuasively: 'We'll find a way.'

I went and had a word with Peter. He agreed. We had horrible visions of our audience, not all in the first bloom of youth, tripping over each other in the flower beds and falling in piles.

'What if it rains?' I said to Fred, thinking this would settle the matter.

'This is France. It won't rain, surely.'

I looked at him pityingly. Rain! The freak storms we had in this region could float an average Ark.

We had a bit of an argy-bargy about this and Fred went off down the garden to have another consolatory cigarette. I went back to the breakfast room. Fuelled with coffee the singers had woken up. They all seemed to be talking at once. I tried a cough but couldn't make myself heard. I resorted to thumping on the table and when they came to a halting stop, risked making myself unpopular by delivering a few house rules. No smoking in the house. And a few things like meal times and where the rubbish went. And would everyone please carry their plates etc. out into the kitchen for stacking in the dishwasher. I caught myself sounding horribly schoolmistressy, so finished rather lamely hoping they'd have a nice day.

They trouped out like lambs and disappeared to their rooms. 'You've put the fear of god in them,' remarked Peter.

'Oh dear I hope not,' I remembered Donna's timid entrance the night before. Maybe he was right.

Mid-morning Fred was still pacing round the garden ominously making notes. Peter left for Moulins to pick up Jane the mezzo-soprano and producer, so key to the whole enterprise – the one who had missed the plane the day before. She had somehow managed to get on a crack of dawn flight and was taking the train down from Paris.

By lunchtime there was still no sign of any rehearsing. Fred was looking depressed and the cast had taken to playing a disconsolate game of football on the lawn. I made a buffet lunch for them. This was meant to be a simple affair to keep them going until the main meal of the day in the evening when they could relax after rehearsing. Ham, pâté, cheese, bread and salads were set out in the kitchen and they all had to help themselves and take a plate out into the garden. It soon became clear that we were going to have to drastically up our bread quota. Kitty in particular could put away six thick slices and still counting.

At three that afternoon, I heard Peter's car return and the sound of female footsteps tip-tapping across the hallway. In came Jane, sashaying across in high heels and little short skirt more suitable for a nightclub than a gravel drive. She greeted me with a gorgeous smile and apology for missing the plane, caused apparently by a massive hangover - all said with an apologetic giggle.

I warmed to her immediately and she'd clearly won Peter over. During their drive home he'd explained the problem about Fred's plan to locate the opera in and around the house and Jane had promised to sort the whole thing out.

As soon as she'd dumped her suitcase in her room she went down the garden to find Fred. Peter and I watched anxiously from an upper window as they walked back and forth clearly discussing the options. We were, I realised, in a position of strength and I felt a little guilty forcing our opinion on them. But we also had a hundred guests to entertain, I needed the downstairs rooms for my champagne reception and buffet. For all we knew the singing might be crap but at least the performance would be out of the way up in the attic and we could have a decent party down below.

I went back to the kitchen to tidy up the lunch and found the singers had stacked the dishwasher and sponged down the table for me. Nice.

Later that afternoon we'd won - the singers were up in the attic. Jane - the diplomat – had sorted the whole thing out. Peter and I slipped out into the courtyard. The attic dormers were open meaning we could listen discreetly down below without being seen. It was a tense moment, would the singers be up to scratch? We heard the opening notes of Marriage of Figaro Act Two on the piano and then a soprano voice, clear as running water, strong and touchingly young. It was Donna singing 'Porgi Amor', the Countesses' poignant aria in which she laments her husband's infidelity. Her voice rang out into the stillness of the fresh country air. I turned to Peter, I think we both had tears in our eyes. It was going to be all right. Actually, it was going to be far better than all right.

We heard Donna's story from Fred. She came from a family where classical music was seldom played. She attended the comprehensive school where Fred taught music and drama and at fifteen she'd auditioned for the school choir. Fred had been stunned by her voice. It was totally untrained but she had a strong soprano voice with a range that reached effortlessly up to the highest notes. With some work she would cover the lower ones too. Above all she was instinctively musical. She was totally unaware of this gift and amazed when Fred suggested that she should audition for Bedfordshire Youth Opera. She didn't know anything about opera. She had never been to an opera. So when she was given a role in 'La Voce di Perdono' she wasn't sure if she wanted to take it. The trip to France had been another hurdle. Her parents were, unsurprisingly, reluctant to allow a sixteen-year-old to go off to France with her schoolmaster and a troupe of unknown singers. For all they knew these people in their grand-sounding French house might be pornographers.

Later that afternoon Peter and I were invited up to the attic to watch the rest of the rehearsal and found Kitty on stage singing 'Voi che sapete' - Cherubino's bashful serenade to the Countess on whom he has a massive crush. Kitty it turned out, not only had a fabulous voice, rounder and fuller and with more volume that Donna and equally musical but she was also a fine actress. Even without the breeches and pigtail, once she started to sing, she became the shy young male who had just discovered the thrill of the opposite sex.

Leo, our younger daughter, arrived that evening from London with her current boyfriend Baz – a handsome tanned sporty type whom we'd known since he was knee-high. Peter was handing kirs round to the cast and I was busy in the kitchen with Pam making Pam's speciality - a one metre square moussaka - when they arrived. Leo and Baz instantly slotted in. Leo was soon having a heart-to-heart with Jane and Baz had been taken off to have a game of frisbee in the park by Roland.

Dinner was another of those multiple-helping meals. I'd bought four kilos of mince and Pam had spent the entire afternoon 'cooking-off' the aubergine. She'd topped it with a couple of pints of cheesey egg custard. At the end of the meal the whole square metre had disappeared. There wasn't even a second helping for Marjorie, she'd have to speed up if she was going to keep up with this lot.

Fred had got into gear by now and wanted the cast to continue rehearsing after dinner. The lot of them had made their way up to the attic. Baz had gone to knock a golf ball around on the lawn. Marjorie had tottered off to bed. Leo, Pam, Juliet and I were clearing up.

'They're all pretty young,' commented Leo. 'What are you doing about sleeping arrangements? Isn't it a bit of a responsibility?'

'Oh, I've got that sorted,' I said. 'Girls on one side of the house and the boys in a kind of dormitory on the other. They'd have to cross the entire house to co-habit.'

Leo paused, tea-towel in hand: 'Mu-um?'

'What?'

She rolled her eyes: 'Haven't you noticed something?'

'No, what?'

'Most of the boys are gay.'

'O-hh?'

'Honestly Mummy.'

'Well, how was I to know? I asked them to list their dietary requirements not their sexual preferences.'

'Well, I'm not letting Baz play frisbee with Roland after dark.'

'He should be safe enough. I've put you and Baz on the girls' side of the house.'

I think I mentioned earlier the layout of the house and the fact that all the bedrooms interconnected. In order to get from one side of the house to the other, any male would have to go through our bedroom and Juliet's bedroom then over the landing and into the girls' side. And vice versa

That night all of us, excluding the singers, retired to bed at a reasonable hour. The cast was still rehearsing when we went up, so Peter left a couple of bottles of red wine and some glasses on the table.

'I dare say they'd like a glass of wine when they finish,' he said.

Exhausted from our first day of running a mass canteen we fell into a deep sleep. I was awoken at about three am by a strange tapping noise on the door between our bedroom and Juliet's. There were, in fact, two doors between us and her. And between these doors there was a square space rather like a box, which was totally pitch dark when the two doors were closed. I supposed Juliet wanted an aspirin or something.

I called out. 'Come on in. It's OK.'

A voice replied. 'It's me, Roland, I'm lost.'

'OK, I'll put the light on. You can come through.'

I switched it on and the door opened. Through walked Roland with great dignity, totally buck-naked.'

'Well!' I said to Peter.

'Go back to sleep,' he said.

When morning came I found a trail of blood along the wall where Roland had gone through.

'Oh my god, I hope he's all right,' I said to Peter.

Downstairs I found Juliet in the kitchen looking pale.

'Do you think the house is haunted?' she said.

'No, it's the least haunted house I've ever been in. Why?'

'I woke up and saw a strange white shape moving across my room.'

'So what did you do?'

'I pulled the covers over my head and went back to sleep.'

'It was Roland. He got lost and was trying to find the way back to his room.'

'But it was all white.'

'He didn't have any clothes on.'

One by one the singers came down to breakfast, but no Roland. I was getting worried and about to send someone to find him when he appeared.

'The strangest thing happened last night,' he said. 'I went to bed and the next thing I knew, I woke up in the flower bed.'

I looked at him in horror. His room was on the first floor.

'The flowerbed! How did you get there?'

'I don't know. I think I must have fallen out of the window.'

We gathered round him: 'Are you all right?'

'Yes, I think so. My arm's a bit sore.'

'Let me look at it.' I rushed for the first aid kit. He had a load of scratches down his right arm. None too serious. 'Do you think you need an X-ray? Shall I call the Doctor?'

We did all the tests. He could move all his fingers and bend his arm. He protested strongly that he was fine and would let me know if he wasn't.

So we bandaged his arm and tried to work out what had happened.

He said that after waking up in the flowerbed, he walked round the house trying to find a way back in. The kitchen door wasn't locked and knowing he needed to get upstairs he'd headed for the main staircase. His sense of direction had led him through Juliet's room into the box-like area between the two rooms. Closing the door behind him, he'd found himself in total pitch darkness, In panic, he was tapping the walls, trying to find a way out – the rest we knew.

'He must have been very drunk,' said Juliet when he was out of earshot. 'Otherwise he would have hurt himself.'

'My god he's the pianist,' said Peter suddenly realising the implications of the whole thing. 'If there's a problem we should cancel. We won't be able to find a replacement pianist at this late date.'

I was starting to get callous over the stress of the whole thing. 'He should go for an X-ray. Otherwise, if he insists he's all right, we better take his word for it.'

'What I don't understand,' said Peter. 'Is how he got so drunk. I mean, I only left them two bottles of wine. One of them was already started.'

The truth came out later. On one of the runs for cigarettes from the village, the cast had stocked up on vodka, gin and whisky – clearly from now on they were not to be trusted.

Drink wasn't the only thing. Nobly, I was trying to impose a healthy diet on them. They put away masses of bread, cheese and cold meats but vegetables had to be made tempting: potatoes roasted with herbs, beans done with tomato and garlic and I could only get them to eat fruit if I made fruit salad served with ice-cream. Fred, in particular, would only eat the ice cream. Whenever portions of vegetables had been put away I felt a certain triumph. But this was short-lived. On a waste-paper basket run, I discovered they had stashes in their bedrooms. Fred had monster packs of Snickers and chocolate biscuits under his bed and he sneaked a large pot of chocolate spread on to the breakfast table.

The four days that had started so slowly suddenly seemed to go into overdrive. With breakneck rapidity Saturday morning dawned and I threw back the curtains to reveal:

'A clear sky and full sun!' I announced the happy news to Peter.

He'd been watching the weather forecast anxiously. We'd hoped to set out the tables and chairs for the dinner in the courtyard. By the time the audience ate, it would be dark enough to hide the absence of a terrace. I'd put out pots of geraniums and the area would be candle-lit. Hopefully it would look quite magical.

I'd put in a massive order for flowers from the florist. This was, after all, our housewarming, the culmination of over two years' restoration work - I wanted to do the house justice. Artful arrangements of flowers would draw eyes away from the negative points – the loose wires hanging out of the wall waiting for the light fittings and the odd bit of woodwork we hadn't had time to paint.

That morning, a lovely neighbour – Françoise - turned up with an armful of flowers from her garden, much nicer and less tortured-looking than the florist's. Juliet and I set to arranging them. Leo and Baz were given the job of preparing new potatoes for a hundred guests – they didn't need peeling but had to be checked over.

Pam had driven to the supermarket and picked up the ten salmon which she was going to cook at her house. Even Marjorie was given a job, winding a napkin round each set of cutlery.

Peter had come up with the clever, economical scheme of putting the table plan on the back of the programme, thus saving paper and ink. As various phone calls came in during the day – people with flu or bugs or wanting to bring sudden extra guests, he was forced to revise his tables. He stormed back and forth like Basil Fawlty on a bad day, as another drop-out caused yet another reprint. I was on the fifth salad by this time and was heard to mutter under my breath that I didn't care where I sat as long as I could sit.

I'd revised my list of dishes for the buffet. Maybe influenced by the amount of food the cast could put away I'd started to worry about quantities. I'd ordered an extra platter of sliced smoked ham from the butcher. And we had back-up plates of other cold meats and smoked salmon in case Pam's cooked salmon ran out. There was a massive cheese board and a choice of four puddings and I'd even made a special trip to Moulins to buy 'Pailettes d'Or' – the local speciality - dark chocolates with bits of real gold leaf embedded in them. I arranged these on a dish on stand and made them the centrepiece of the table.

The singers had done a timed run-through the night before and rehearsed for an hour in the morning to clear up a few ragged ends. Fred had given them the rest of the day off. We lent four of them a car to go off and visit some local beauty spots. But Fred and Jane and Roland stayed back: Fred smoking furiously and biting his nails – clearly nervous - and Roland trying to persuade Baz to have yet another game of frisbee.

By six the car was back and everyone had retired to their quarters. The hot water was run till it went cold as everyone took showers. But at last, I was dressed and Leo was helping Marjorie get ready. Claudia had turned up in a car with a load of Parisians who were hanging round smoking and generally looking cool and stylish, getting in everyone's way. Pam had arrived with the prepared salmon, dumped them and then disappeared at a key moment. The cats were stalking around the buffet like starved leopards round a herd of wildebeests, waiting for an off-chance for a raid when no-one was looking. Peter was dressed and pacing his study practising his welcome speech – in French. This speech had been composed and rehearsed exhaustively with Corinne - his pretty French teacher. She had even written out the syllables phonetically under each word, so his pronunciation should be perfect.

I was showered, dressed and was wrapped in an apron, just about to portion the salmon out on to the serving plates when Jane came into the kitchen looking fraught.

'Where can I find a bucket?'

I pointed her in the direction of the utility room.

'What for?'

'Dan says he's going to throw up. Too much sun.'

'Is he going to be able to sing?'

She shrugged: 'Hopefully.'

Fred came by at that point. 'Has anyone seen my score?'

'I think you left it on the table in the garden. Why?'

'I need to learn my part.'

Leo put her head round the kitchen door. 'Mu-um, there are people outside. I think the audience is starting to arrive.'

'They're too early. Go and talk to them.'
'I can't, they're French.'
'Send Claudia then.'
'She can't. She's broken the heel off her shoe.'
'Or Pam.'
'She's mending it.'
'Uggghhhhrrr! I'll go myself.'

I shot through the salon only to catch sight of their receding backs. Slightly stuffy backs I recognised as belonging to a family that stretched back to some truncated branch of French royalty – not Bourbons - only Valois. But still…

'I speak French. I told them to take a turn round the garden,' said a voice.

An ostensibly naked Roland was seated on the sofa knitting, his one earring on the door side. From the Valois point of view, there was no way they could have told he was wearing bathing trunks. My reputation in the Departement - which this evening was designed to establish – had gone down another notch.

The arrival of the de Valois seemed to have opened the floodgates. There was the sound of slamming car doors from the orchard. M. Aubertin, was standing in the driveway with his 'P' arm band on, officiously waving the first-comers to the far end. With typical French sang-froid they ignored him and parked higgledy-piggledy wherever they wanted.

The audience came down the driveway in chatting duos and trios, grouping and regrouping with loads of Mwah-mwahing. I shot back into the house and chivvied Jacqueline, our cleaning lady who had brought most of her extended family to help, out to the front of the house. Someone had to start serving the champagne.

Peter and I took up our positions at the front door ready to greet everyone and do the round of introductions. This proved to be totally unnecessary – all our guests knew each other – in fact most of them were related. This was the Allier, where over the centuries, families had intermarried within their close family circle with the dedication of rare breeds. Everyone seemed to be an aunt or nephew or an in-law or to share an 'arrière-grandparent' somewhere down the family line.

The boy who was opening the champagne – nephew of Jacqueline and destined for a career in the police (enough said) -had at last mastered the feat of getting cork out of bottle. Glasses started to circulate and as they did so, the sound of voices rose a few semitones. Whatever was about to take place in the attic, the audience seemed to be enjoying themselves. I popped upstairs to see how the cast was getting on. Dan emerged from the bathroom, pale but bucketless. Fred was sitting on the floor muttering over his score. One of the sopranos was worryingly asking for throat sweets.

'Don't take any notice,' said Fred without looking up. 'Singers' nerves, she'll be fine when she gets on stage.'

'Good luck everyone. Break legs arms whatever. Don't worry about a thing. We're getting them all totally pissed on champagne. They'll love it.'

I took a sneak glance through the upstairs landing window, trying to estimate how many guests had arrived so far. The promised time for the 7.00pm start was nearly upon us. I could see Peter below taking his speech out of an inside pocket and having a furtive glance at it. He moved into position in front of the doorway.

No one was taking any notice of him. Long lost friends and distant cousins were catching up on the past year. Peter tried tapping a glass. No reaction.

I hurried down to the hallway and caught two children and sent them up the tower staircase to ring the bell in the tower. This similarly had no effect. Only when Peter had climbed on to a coffee table and shouted a 'Bridget Jones' type 'OY', did they come to a halting silence.

He unfolded his speech and delivered his welcome, reading his perfectly rehearsed phonetics. The fact that, ever after, our guests believed Peter spoke impeccable French, and greeted him wherever he went with long and fast French dialogues, of which he understood not a word, was an unfortunate side effect.

We did eventually get the audience up into the attic. They listened to the first act with rapt attention. I'm not sure how much the French understood of this ingenious and witty reworking of Mozart's plots.

None of them had had time to read the French synopsis, they'd all been far too busy talking to each other. In fact, chatting to French friends later, I discovered each of them had a totally different version of the story. But opera plots are pretty barmy anyway - what mattered was the singing.

Kitty charmed everyone with her Cherubino aria and although Donna never dared to raise her eyes from the attic floor, she made up for it with her voice which was divine. Of course Fred remembered his lines, after all he'd written most of them.

The act ended to resounding applause. I caught Pam's eye as we led the audience downstairs for our next trial by jury – the meal.

'We're British, so they won't be expecting much,' whispered Pam.

But British or not, the food seemed to go down a treat. Admittedly, the dinner was somewhat chaotic as the French had no idea how to handle a buffet and didn't take kindly to lining up in a queue. Having, at last, achieved the ultimate goal of the table, they piled everything on to their plates at the same time, from salmon through to trifle and chocolates, but 'tant pis – zis is 'ow ze English eat, no?'

Once they were seated in the candlelit courtyard, the conversations, which had been so abruptly interrupted by the opera, struck up again. The dinner interval stretched from its predicted hour through another half hour as they went back for yet another glass of wine and maybe just a 'leetle' more cheese - and yet another half hour as they formed queues for the loos. It took forever to herd them back upstairs for the second half of the opera and I think we might have lost one or two on the way, as I heard cars on the move in the orchard.

Warmed by the food and wine, the second half had an even better reception with noisy clapping after every aria. As the final quartet came to a close, I gazed out through the dormer as the moon rose behind the vast Sequoia tree at the end of the park. They'd done it. We'd done it! I'll never hear that final aria from Figaro 'La Voce di Perdono', without remembering that moment and the applause that followed. Our new floorboards rocked to the stamping, and dust descended in clouds to the floors beneath.

The last guests had gone. I'd made the rounds of the tables in the courtyard snuffing out the candles. The singers, plus the younger generation of guests had disappeared to the end of the garden with blankets and bottles and i-pods and were having a celebration party.

Peter and I went up to bed. I was far too strung up to sleep. My mind was racing. Infuriatingly I could hear Peter's steady breathing. Then he turned over.

'Are you asleep?'

'I was.'

'It was all right, wasn't it?'

'They were brilliant.'

'I think the guests enjoyed it.'

'Bloody well should have.'

'So we could do it again next year?'

'What?' He was wide awake now. 'I thought this was just for our house-warming.'

'No, but Figaro. That was the whole point. To do the whole opera - The Marriage of Figaro, in this house.'

'Too difficult. They're too young.'

'Donna could do it. So could Kitty and Jane.'

'And think of the cost.'

'It can't've cost that much, we did everything ourselves.'

'Their fares, the food and the wine!'

'How much did it cost?'

'Dread to think. I haven't added it up yet.'

'Maybe we could get someone else to chip in. A second performance somewhere. There must be someone. Then we could share the costs.'

'In English?'

'They don't have to sing in English.'

'Anyway. Who?'

'I'll think about it.'

By morning, accolades were coming in via the internet. Peter had been up in his office checking his email while I laid the table for breakfast. He came down looking very pleased with himself.

'Smashing email from Piggy. (One of his clients).'
'Oh?'
'Wants to know if we're doing it next year.'
Me (non-committally) 'But think of the expense.'
'Well, if we could find someone to share the costs...'

He went back up to his office with a cup of coffee. I could hear him on the phone having one of those blokey conversations.

'Oh right.. guffaw guffaw... No, really? .....(silence and listening)... Guffaw, guffaw... Not a bit of it...falling off a log...slice of cake...'

'Hmmm.'

Later that morning I was stacking the dishwasher when I heard Peter say:

'Fred. Can we have a word with you?'

Fred was on his second slice of toast and Nutella and looking distinctly the worse for wear. The cast had had a bit of a party. In fact, I don't think some of them had been to bed at all. I wondered if they were going to manage the drive up to Paris for their flight later that day. I gave Fred another cup of coffee and we followed him outside for his first fag of the morning.

I wondered what Peter was going to say. A big 'thank you' no doubt and a bit of a pep talk. But to my amazement I heard instead: 'The thing is. Do you think you could do The Marriage of Figaro for us. Next year?'

'You mean it? You want us to come again?' Fred had tears in his eyes.

'Of course we do.' I took the coffee cup from him. His hands were shaking.

'The Marriage of Figaro?'

'Yes.'

'You wouldn't prefer something lighter? A little Night Music? Cabaret. Music theatre is really my thing.'

I shook my head and said firmly: 'No it has to be Figaro.'

'I'll have to think about it. I'm not sure if I can get the voices.'

'But you have already. Kitty, Donna, Jane...'

'I suppose I could play the Count,' he said brightening.

We waved them off later that morning knowing that if everything went well they would be back next year. 'The Voce di Perdono' had been a trial run as far as I was concerned, it was just an overture - a dress rehearsal - for the real thing.

Chapter Eight

A year has to pass before they can come again. Normality returns to Gozinière. The bed-linen and towels are washed and back in the linen cupboard, The tablecloths have had the candle wax rinsed out of them with boiling water, the wine-stains have been bleached with St Marc and they're ironed and back in the drawers. The piles of Limoges china have been sorted and stacked in the cupboard. A forest of knives and forks are in elastic-banded clumps and the glasses have been cling-filmed into boxes and are up in the attic. All of it is put away awaiting next year's opera.

September is upon us almost before we know it. The shadows are longer and have an inky depth to them. The nights are drawing in and cold, in the morning the lawns are drenched with dew and fairy circles of field mushrooms have shot up for our breakfast.

The men have, at last, arrived to put in the new terrace. It is like a big U following the internal shape of the house enclosed by the two wings. The acoustics should be good, the walls of the house forming a natural arena. Already I can picture the terrace as a stage with the audience arranged in rows in the centre. Peter comments that the far end of the courtyard now looks a little bare and on one of his trips to Switzerland he discovers an architectural salvage merchant in Mâcon who has various statues and gazebos that could form a feature.

Pam steps in to look after Marjorie so that I can accompany Peter on a few of his business trips. He's treated himself to a fast little two-seater Peugeot, various called his 'aspirateur de femmes' (Hoover of women) or 'hairdresser's car' depending on who's doing the teasing. On one of our trips to Vevey, the little Peugeot takes a breather at Mâcon while we search through the salvage merchant's fascinating hoard of rescued items. Here you can buy an entire 18th Century stone floor or a marble bath or a set of matching terracotta statues of women with sheaves of corn and men with scythes fashioned with post-Revolutionary fervour in the early 1800's. We fall for a lovely stone well with a decorative cast iron cage for its bucket on chain – it's perfect for Gozinière - which can't quite make its mind up whether it's a functional farmhouse or an elegant nobleman's pad. I ask Madame, the owner of the shop, how we can to get it home. She says 'no problem', she'll send it as a part-load next time there's a lorry going in our direction. We pay for the well plus the delivery charge and make our way on to Switzerland. I wonder if we'll ever see the well again. Who in the world is going to be coming to the Allier with a load of architectural salvage?

Back home after the business trip, we stand and admire our Loire stone terrace and open a bottle of champagne with the mason who chinks his glass to ours looking shy and proud at the same time. The workmen here can't quite get used to our English casual friendliness. We are starting to learn about the caste system of this backward region. You can't just mix people up together as we do in Britain. We once invited the locals to a disastrous Christmas Eve party with mulled wine and mince pies. The French expected the pies to be savoury and the wine to be cold and were clearly embarrassed at who they had been invited with.

For my taste the terrace is a bit too perfect and a bit too new. I plan to pour spaghetti water over it to encourage moss to grow. It has worked a treat on the garden statues, one of which M. Aubertin has painstakingly cleaned while I was away.

But will our terrace ever serve as a stage? Fred hasn't promised anything yet, but emails are flying back and forth between Peter and Jane. Jane is out of a job, and impressed by her diplomacy and organisational skills, Peter has arranged an interview for her with a branch of his old ad. agency in Dublin. They snap her up. I'm glad for her but worried that she'll be too busy and maybe too far from the others based in Bedfordshire, to organise Figaro.

Fred has gone back to his teaching job in Donna's school but we have news that he and Roland and a third chap have been given a spot, covering for someone who has dropped out, on the Jonathon Ross Show. It's called 'Three Pouffs and a Piano'. Isolated as we are out in Central France, we never manage to see it.

I ring him up to congratulate him. He says it's an exciting opportunity but causing slight problems at school.

Me: How come?

Fred: Well, there's a particularly irritating pupil of mine who got up in front of the class and said. 'Didn't I see you on the tele last night, Mr Broom?' 'You could well have done.' 'Yeah. It was called 'Three Pouffs and a piana'. 'And?' 'The thing is - you ain't a piana, are you, Mr Broom?' He dissolves into giggles at the other end of the line.

Autumn is fading into winter. The oaks in the forest have turned from gold, to rust, to russet and the last leaves are falling. Our hunts for cèpes which yielded kilos in October are coming to an end. Winter is upon us and the trees stand stark and leafless in the park.

'I wonder why it doesn't snow,' says Marjorie gazing out of the window. I don't dare tell her that it's actually too cold to snow. The thermometer is registering -4C. Peter has flown off for a meeting somewhere warm and sunny and far too important for me to accompany him. I drag huge logs in from the woodpile and build massive fires in the breakfast room. This has become the only room we use now. Marjorie, the cats and I spend a lot of time roasting ourselves in front of the leaping flames.

One morning I get a call from a rough-sounding fellow who says he's on his way to our house from Clermont Ferrand. I tell him he must have the wrong number but he rings again and insists he has a delivery for me of a '....' (I miss the crucial word because of the bad line).

'A what?'

'A puis.' I rack my brain for what a 'puis' is.

'En pierre!' he shouts between more interference.

Pierre – 'stone' my brain registers.

'Oh un puits!' A well! The penny has dropped.

'Have you got a crane?' he shouts.

'No.'

'Have you got anyone strong there to help unload it?'

'No, I'm alone here with my mother. She's ninety-three.'

There's a lot a muffled complaining the other end.

'Then I'll have to take it back again. Back to Mâcon,' he says.

'No, don't do that. I'll think of something. Give me your number.'

'What's going on?' comes from the fireside.
'There's a man in a lorry trying to deliver a well.'
'A what?' says Marjorie.
'A well.'
'What do you want a well for, you've got mains water?'

I give up. I go up to my study and stare at the wall. Where on earth am I going to get a crane from? Or a strong man? Maybe two strong men. I rack my brains and come up with the mason. But he's not coming for a couple of days because he's run out of cement. The cement is due to be delivered from the local builders' merchant but it hasn't come yet. Builders' merchant! They have to cart heavy stuff around, just maybe… It's worth a try. I race for the telephone directory and phone Point P. I get a nice-sounding fellow on the other end.

'This may sound absolutely mad, but I've got a man coming from Clermont Ferrand in a lorry. Do you have a crane we could borrow? He's got a well for me. It's very heavy?'

'A what?' (Here we go again).

'A well. It's stone.'

He asks for my name and address. 'But Madame, we already have a delivery for you.'

'Yes, I know. Cement.'

'Then that's simple. Get your man to deliver the well to me and I'll bring it to you with your cement. Our lorry has a crane on board.'

I couldn't be hearing this. Thanking him profusely, I ring the man in the lorry. He does a lot more muttering as I explain where Point P is and he asks about payment. I tell him that the payment has already been made to the salvage yard. More telephone calls fly back and forth.

'Is it dinner time?' asks Marjorie.

I'm just serving the dinner when we hear rumbling lorry noises coming from the parking area. My precious well has arrived, except it doesn't look in the least like a well. It looks like three palettes with a load of old stones heavy-duty cling-filmed to them. Even the cast iron arch has been disassembled and packed flat. The palettes are swung out from the lorry and placed gently on the gravel. The cement sacks are plonked down beside them. I peer through the protective plastic and note that at least the stones are numbered.

I have my purse with me and ask the delivery man how much I owe him.

He waves this off with a hand. 'I was coming here anyway,' he says.

English people moan about the French, particularly Parisians but I can never get over the kindness we've found as foreigners and complete strangers in this region.

The mason turns up next day and I find him staring at the palettes sucking through his teeth.

'What's this lot then?'

'It's a well. An antique well. Do you think you can put it together?'

He rips some of the plastic back and does some more teeth-sucking. 'What are these numbers then? English?'

I follow his gaze. X. XII. XVI. 'No, they're Roman.'

'So, it's a Roman well?'

'No, it's just the way they're numbered.' I explain the numerals.'

Fortunately, we have a spell of mild weather at this point. The mason leaves his men, who I've secretly nicknamed 'Clueless', 'Feckless' and 'Legless' to put the well together. It takes two days and I'm called out to see the splendid last moment when they cement its decorative iron topknot into place. The original holes are still there, bored into the rim of stones, so they can't go wrong. Except it won't fit. There's a lot of consternation. I take a look inside the well and spot the cause of the problem – they've got their XI where they should have their IX. The cement has already dried so there's no way they can switch them round now. The mason mutters something about posey salvage merchants and bores two new holes and the cage goes on.

I stand back – beautiful! Now all I have to do is fill it with water and get some lilies and goldfish.

I'm wondering how we can work a well into the plot of The Marriage of Figaro. We've had hopeful emails from Fred saying he's found a tenor who'll be great for Figaro and he's working on adapting the score. Would it be all right if we paid for the Tippex?

'What's all this about Tippex?' asks Peter.

I shrug. I hadn't thought about the problems of providing nine or ten scores. 'I suppose he needs to alter a few things.' The bill for Tippex adds up to £100 but to compensate Jane manages to get the photocopying and binding done cheaply at work.

What about the costumes? I'm on the phone again to Fred. Fred's decided to set Figaro in the 1920's – a bit of a blow because I wanted it to be in the 18th Century. But he's adamant about it, he's rewritten an update of the dialogue and it's too late to change now. I think of the weight of Tippex he's already used and back down. Apparently, Fred has a couple of friends who can make the costumes for practically nothing. All we have to do is pay for the fabric and give them another £100 or so for their work. I send him another cheque. My cheque book is looking very thin. I start raiding our joint account. The bills are still coming in for the renovation of the house and the girls are making noises about wanting a swimming pool.

'Honestly Mummy, there's absolutely nothing for my friends to do when they come down here,' moans Claudia. I feel like retorting that 'nothing' seems to be what her friends like doing best, but I suppose you can pose better by a pool.

I call up a swimming pool supplier. Peter is somewhere in Central America and has left it to me to make the decisions on the house. He's actually staying in a five-star hotel and getting a tan between meetings. Marjorie and I huddle round the fire in the evenings and generally Pam comes to join us for supper. The garden is bleak and silent, the only thing that moves is the occasional tractor going by, its revolving light glimmering through the hedge. When I moan about this to Peter on the phone he feels rightfully guilty. He's also earning quite a lot of money.

'Oh go ahead if you think we need it,' he says airily. 'It'll be useful to cool off in the summer. And lovely for the singers.'

'You spoil them.'

'They spoil us.'

The swimming pool man and I pace out a rough rectangle in a corner of a frosty meadow well away from the house. There used to be a house here once and a couple of retaining walls are still standing. I suggest we incorporate them into a poolhouse.

'Tout a fait. Tout a fait.' he says. He does a big flattery job, praising my French and telling me I've cleverly chosen the ideal spot. It's a raised area that actually has a lovely view over the countryside and vitally it doesn't have any deciduous trees around it.

'No leaves to fall in the water.'

'Tout a fait,' he agrees.

Nothing is too difficult for this wonder boy of swimming pool science. The fact that it's mid-winter and I'm the only client he's had in months no doubt helps.

His estimate comes back within days. It doesn't look too bad. I relay the news to Peter and pile it on a bit about what a miserable winter we're having – more guilt results in a 'yes' and I sign the poolman's estimate with a 'bon pour accord' flourish before Peter can change his mind.

The swimming pool company are due to start work in May, after 'Sans Gel' - the magical day when we can be sure the last frosts are well and truly over - and they certainly know how to do frost here. We woke up one morning to minus16C and when I turned the tap on, no water came out. The plumber came and announced that the mains water pipe had frozen. A problem he quickly solved with a hairdryer on an extension lead. As compensation when the sun broke through the mist later that morning we found all the trees were covered in a mantle of glittering ice that tinkled when you walked underneath. Stunning.

But winter is passing. Pam and I note the lengthening days as each one brings another precious minute of daylight. March comes at last. One morning I open my study window and a blast of fresh warm air sweeps in. It smells damp and mossy and I can hear a strange burbling cry coming from the sky. Leaning out of the window, I spot a long straggling arrow of cranes overhead. They pass in formation, calling to each other with their strange creaking cries. All through the day I watch long arrows of cranes crossing our land. Spring has arrived.

By April wild flowers leap into life in the meadows, thousands of cowslips, fragile blue flowers that must be the ancestors of our present day cornflowers and some evil-looking mauve orchids with spotted leaves. When I walk through the long grass I kick up a surf of butterflies.

Peter is back home and working like a trooper on the allotment. He and M. Aubertin have got out the rotavator and are ploughing up the heavy clotted soil. M. Aubertin is given the job of raking and levelling and taking out the weed roots. Then Peter enrols me in my annual job of dropping potatoes as he digs the holes. M. Aubertin watches us from the sidelines with a look of amusement on his face. It's back-breaking work and we pause for a well-earned coffee. When we return to the plot we find he's finishing off our work. He's found some sort of medieval implement with a long handle – a cross between a spade and a hoe - and he's forming a trench with it, working backwards, dropping a potato from his pocket at regular intervals and letting the soil fall back naturally to cover it, in one swift economical movement.

We both watch impressed. He stands back, looking very pleased with himself as he comes to the end of the row. Peter mutters something to me about the potatoes not being in deep enough and goes to check his email. I congratulate M.Aubertin on his work.

'Peter would have taken hours over that.'

'Oh, but just think,' he says. 'Monsieur. He does office work!'

When it came to the swimming pool bill, and all the extras plus the poolhouse, which had to be totally reconstructed from the two extant walls (in fact it would have been simpler to start from scratch) I had to admit that M. Aubertin had a point. It was Peter's office work that was paying for it all.

'And as you said, it's going to be wonderful for the singers,' I point out as we receive an eye-watering bill for filling up the pool.

Chapter Nine

We'd planned to stage the opera earlier this year, on the first Saturday in August, when we should be certain of the weather. Our Loire stone terrace/stage is now looking a little more weathered after its first winter. The road builders have been back with lorry loads of gravel for the centre of the courtyard. The well now looks splendid surrounded by the creamy, golden gravel and the plumbers have installed a water supply inside. We fill it and I drive to Moulins to buy the water lilies and goldfish.

June arrives and the news from the U.K. is that Figaro has been cast. We're sent the cast list and Peter starts looking into cheap flights to Paris. After last year's fiasco with the hire cars he decides to book them on the train from Paris down to Moulins.

We start work on the programme. Claudia, the graphic designer of the family, is given the job of designing it. Peter looks up the synopsis in friend Charles Osborne's 'The Complete Operas of Mozart'. French teacher Corinne, is employed to translate this into French. I suggest to Peter that we send our French guests the programme in advance to give them time to mug up on the story before they arrive. Peter and I put our heads together over the guest list. Some of the stuffier guests from last year are substituted by new people we've met more recently.

Peter is still making noises about finding a second venue for the opera, it seems a crime that the cast should come all this way and put in so much work and only have one performance.

I have my own idea about this. The previous summer Peter had got into conversation with Marc Terray, who ran an excellent bookshop in Moulins with the help of his extremely attractive wife. His English was excellent, having been sent to boarding school in England. Marc was a Parisian who had thrown up a career in Paris in order to come down to Allier and renovate what had been his family's ancestral home for over seven centuries. This was a 16th Century chateau with an unusual Italianate façade, poised on a hillside three or so kilometres outside Moulins. Over the past couple of centuries it had fallen into disrepair and recently been used by a farmer as a kind of storehouse. I immediately recognised in Marc a fellow Housaholic (a person like me who has a quite irrational love of houses) or in his case one house in particular. We were keen customers of the Terray's bookshop as they supplied classical music CD's as well as books – hard to find elsewhere in the Allier.

On one of our visits to the shop, Marc had told us they were having a Georges Sand evening at their chateau. A group of actors were performing in their courtyard, complete with a working carriage and pair. I'd been dying to take a closer look at their house which I'd had tantalizing glimpses of in the distance, on my trips to and from Moulins. So in spite of the fact that neither of us spoke good enough French to understand much of what would take place on stage, we went along. Our lack of French was compensated for by sitting under a starlit sky with the actors playing against a backdrop of the chateau's ornate façade.

Since they'd staged this performance the year before, quite possibly they might be interested in our singers this year. But I couldn't simply ring them up and blurt it out on the phone – particularly in my challenged French.

An excuse cropped up unexpectedly. Peter and I were invited to a First Communion. I needed advice on a suitable present and the Terray's were the obvious people to give it. I put on rather better clothes than usual and drove to Moulins. Arriving in the shop, neither Marc, nor his wife Laurence was around. I snooped among the children's books and then just as I was giving up, a lovely deep throaty voice asked: 'Can I help you?' Laurence appeared out of the back of the shop. I explained the problem and we went through several books settling eventually on a big illustrated children's encyclopedia. While she was wrapping it, I thanked her for the 'Georges Sand' evening.

'Yes, well Marc wasn't too happy with it. We're trying to find something else to put on this year.'

I could hardly believe my ears.

'As a matter of fact, we're planning a musical evening this summer: an opera 'The Marriage of Figaro'. Perhaps you and your husband would like to come?'

'You must be the English people who put on an opera last year?'

Of course she'd heard of us. In the Allier news travels from 'bouche a l'oreille' mouth-to-ear as they say in France, at lightning speed. We were soon deep in a discussion over the ins and outs of staging a home-based performance.

'You don't think your singers might be willing to do something for us?' she finished.

Tah-dah!

We arranged for the Terray's to come over for a drink and see the video footage Pam had shot of 'La Voce di Perdono'. Peter was suspiciously enthusiastic about the invitation – I think this might have something to do with Laurence's gorgeous gravelly voice (and that smile!).

Their visit ended with Marc saying they were more than happy with the singers and would like to arrange something and would be in touch. Laurence kissed me on both cheeks and saying in her delicious accent: 'I'm so glad we've met. I lurve Pe-ter.'

'Hmmm.!'

It turned out that they didn't want an opera but through various emails back and forth between ourselves and Fred and Roland, it was agreed that the singers would put together an evening of arias, quartets and trios for them.

So, we had a second performance, the programmes were in production, the invitations were being sent out and Pam and I were planning the menu. Hopefully these friends of Fred were busily churning out the costumes. All we needed now was a fine night in August.

The weather was extremely unsettled that July. Freak storms hit out of nowhere every few days. You could tell when they were coming: dark clouds would mass overhead, there would be an ominous stillness - as if nature was holding its breath - birds would cease to sing, crickets fall silent - then a flash and rumble would be followed by a wind that swept through the landscape at up to 100 kilometres per hour. It tore through the park, howling in the attic, ripping branches off the trees and sending gusts heavy with torn leaves into every pocket and corner of the house. The wind would be followed by torrential rain. It came down like a power shower soaking the lawns and leaving puddles on the gravel. Then the storm would stop as abruptly as it had started and the sun would come out.

These storms were dangerous too. Allier lightning was nothing like tame British lightning. It had a ferocity that sent it forking down from the sky to hit the ground; one bolt killed our neighbour's horse and put out the entire local electricity supply for two days. We'd learned to take precautions. As soon as we heard the first rumble we'd got into a routine of unplugging our computers and television, but we didn't always remember everything. One morning after a particularly fierce storm, I came downstairs to find my sewing machine eerily sewing by itself at a speed that burnt out its motor.

As August approached we scanned the long range weather forecast anxiously. The piano we used was electric, so no electricity meant no accompaniment. Torrential rain would put paid to staging the opera on our brand new terrace and have us up in the attic again.

The travel arrangements were proving to be a nightmare. Peter had booked the flights to Paris on a British credit card and these had been delivered to Jane. Then at the last minute one of the cast pulled out. Since the tickets were all for individually named people, Peter had to book a new ticket for the new singer. The rail tickets were also problematic. SNCF would only be paid with a French card and the tickets could only be sent to the billing address of the card holder. To be extra safe, Peter drove to the station and picked up the tickets, then he put them in an envelope securely sellotaped down and posted them to Jane.

'Did you register the package,' I asked.

'No but I photocopied all the tickets so if they go astray, I've got reference.'

'Should be OK then.'

As the day of travel approached Peter was getting more and more anxious. Jane kept emailing saying the tickets hadn't arrived. When there was a mere three days to go Peter decided to drive to Moulins with his photocopies and cancel the tickets and buy new ones. 'No problem to cancel the tickets,' said the woman behind the guichet as Peter forked out another 500 euros. 'As soon as you get the other tickets back, bring them in here and I'll give you a refund.'

'But what if they never arrive?' said Peter (or something vaguely similar in French).

'Then you don't get a refund.'

'But these seats have been cancelled. You can resell them.'

After a few attempts to rephrase this, she understood and admitted it was true. But 'no tickets, no refund' - that was the rule.

It has taken us some time to come to terms with the fact that France is a country where, if you can cheat, people will cheat. Organisations such as France's nationalised rail company - the SNCF - arm themselves against fare dodgers with draconian rules.

Peter came back from Moulins positively steaming. He'd go higher he stormed, he'd write to the bloody Chairman of SNCF!!

'But the tickets may still turn up,' I said placatingly.

They didn't. In fact they never turned up. And Peter did write to the bloody Chairman and amazingly he got a reply: 'No tickets, no refund'. Had Peter still been young enough and nimble enough to jump barriers, another fare dodger would have joined the ranks of France's travel cheats.

At last the first of August dawned, the entire cast caught the plane and that afternoon Peter set off with a kind friend and a borrowed trailer to pick them up from Moulins station. Pam and I had a large supper ready. We needed to get into the swing of things, we'd be feeding fourteen at every meal for the week to come.

The cars arrived and I ran to the front door to welcome the cast. Jane and Fred first, both running to me for a hug. Donna hanging back but looking a lot less shy than last year. Kitty as lovely as ever and Dan, who was standing in for the fellow who had dropped out at the last minute, had come to play Figaro. But there were new people to be introduced. A slender dark girl, a little older than the others, Helen, who was to play the Countess, Tom, a tall strong looking youth with a wonderful London accent who was to double up as Dr Bartolo and the drunken gardener and finally Nic Gibney – slim dark, with drop-dead gorgeous blue eyes who was soon to be adopted as La Gozinière's resident pet. Lastly, Kate, the stage manager, a pretty blonde who, rather alarmingly, was walking with the aid of a crutch. She had broken her leg and had just come out of plaster. I wondered how on earth she was going to manage carting lights and scenery around?

We were far more organised this year. We'd put up an easel with a notice board in the hall. I'd drawn a floor-plan of the house showing where each person would be sleeping. Peter had done a sheet listing meal-times and House Rules – a few important ones had been added this year like 'no glasses to be taken to the swimming pool' and 'please keep the cats out of the pantry'. The board would be used for Rehearsal Schedules and Peter's all-important daily weather forecast.

By six the cast had settled into their rooms and were down in the courtyard having a kir and getting to know us. Marjorie arrived in a stately fashion with her walker and became the focus of attention. She'd always loved young people. Having escaped the confines of her apartment block in Bexhill, where the youngest occupant was at least eighty, she was revelling in the fact of being surrounded by youth.

'Oh yes, I've been on the stage. My late husband was very good….' I overheard her telling someone about her Amateur Dramatic performances in Devon. 'I've still got the photos, black and white, of course. I'll see if I can dig them out…'

It has been a hot day and the evening is blissfully warm. We get the boys to put two garden tables end to end and eat outside. As the sun goes down behind the tower, the conversation divides into natural groups. Peter is sounding Jane out about various clients, colleagues and intrigues in his old agency. Kitty and Helen are comparing notes on different divas. I move down the table, I want to get to know Kate, we're going to have to join forces on the props, lighting and the minimal scenery.

'I hope it's not going to be too much for you.' I say, eyeing her crutch.

'Don't worry about that,' she said. 'I need the exercise.'

It turns out she knows what she's talking about. She's a physiotherapist working in a senior position at Charing Cross Hospital.

A fact that proves handy later in the week. Kate loves singing and belongs to a London choir, she also plays the flute. In addition to being stage manager she'll turn pages for Roland, a task we'd given to a neighbouring piano teacher the year before.

The meal comes to an end, but no-one seems anxious to leave the table apart from Marjorie who has already invited members of the cast round to her little apartment for drinks tomorrow. I just hope she doesn't get them too drunk.

The sky above turns from hazy blue to indigo and a web of stars appears overhead. I put candles on the table and Peter fetches a couple more bottles of wine. It's time to clear the table. I do so as discreetly as possible so as not to disturb the conversation. Pam and I are finishing loading the dishwasher when Nic appears in the kitchen. The sink is full of things that we can't fit in - saucepans mostly.

'Oh I'll do this,' he says. 'I just love washing saucepans.'

'Nobody loves washing saucepans,' I counter.

'Oh I do. It gives me real satisfaction. Now, have you got one of those little knitted steel scrubber thingees. Yes, you have. Pass it over. Now you two go and sit down with the others. You've done all the cooking.'

As I said, Nic was heading for pet status.

The year before, 'La Voce di Perdono' had been rehearsed and staged before the singers arrived. This year was a totally different proposition. Few of the singers had even met before they boarded the plane. They had been sent their scores and were meant to have learned their parts and rehearsed their arias with their singing teachers. But the week at Gozinière would be the crucial time in which Fred would develop the production. He had six days to get the opera learnt and blocked. Every movement and every line needed to be rehearsed until it became automatic. The fact that Fred was also singing the part of the Count, made this task even more challenging.

The next morning the cast is down at the appointed breakfast time – nine – but there's no sign of Fred. We have a noisy breakfast and both big loaves we've ordered get eaten. We're clearing the table when Fred arrives, grabs a coffee and goes into the courtyard for his first cigarette of the day.

I catch Pam sneaking out to join him.

'You've given up, remember?'

'But I still smoke the occasional O.P.'

'O.P.?'

'Other peoples'.'

Fred takes the cast up to the attic. I'm just about to stop him and point out we now have a courtyard, when Peter grabs me.

'Leave him to make up his own mind where to stage it,' he says.

'But what about our lovely new terrace?'

'It may rain.'

'It may not.'

The Marriage of Figaro takes place on a single, sunny, summer day. Sunny because it's meant to be set in Spain in the country house of an 18th Century Count. It's the wedding day of Figaro, the Count's barber, and Susanna the Countess's lively and pretty maid. But all is not peace and happiness under its roof. The Count has his eye on the young bride Susanna and although he has officially abolished 'Droit de Seigneur', he'd like to give it just one last fling.

Naturally we're dying to hear the new singers' voices But they don't seem to be rehearsing. We can hear strange bumps and giggles coming through the dormers. Eventually, curiosity gets the better of me and I slip up the spiral staircase to see what's going on. They're doing 'Bonding Exercises' falling to be caught at the last minute in each other's arms. At the point I enter they're sitting in a circle on the floor, deep into memory games. I creep back down again.

'I hope they start rehearsing soon,' I say to Pam. 'They've only got a week.'

Pam shrugs, 'Thank god it's no longer. Think of the food!'

By afternoon we can hear the piano playing but the singers have all dispersed to different corners of the house. Wherever you go you encounter weird warming-up noises:

'Mmmmmmmmmmmm…mmmmmmmmmmmm.'

'Eeee-e-e-e-ee.'

'Brrrrrrrrrrrrrrr-rrrrrr-rrrr-rrrr'

'Mum mum mum mum mum'
'AAAAAAhhhh… AAAAHHHH…AAA.AHHHHHH.'
One of the sopranos in particular is practising arpeggios. Up and up, higher and higher they go, until they sound impossibly high - and then she starts at the bottom again. I find the cats crouching under the stairs, their fur arched up along their backs. The male, Boris, has a tail fluffed out like a bottle-brush. He thinks this wailing noise is the battle cry of some gargantuan tom.

By around mid-afternoon Fred is ready to rehearse Act One. He's decided the first scene will take place in the attic where an area has been marked out to represent Figaro and Susanna's potential bedroom. Kate has found a piece of baton and is busy marking it up as a massive ruler. The cheval mirror has mysteriously disappeared from our bedroom and I've been sent on a search through drawers to find lace and ribbons which can be made into Susanna's wedding headdress.

I hear Dan's voice belting out: 'Five, ten, fifteen, twenty…'

Yes, the opera is to be sung in English. We were originally disappointed that it wouldn't be sung in Italian, but as Fred pointed out, with limited rehearsal time and a young cast, to do the whole opera in Italian would be impossible. We discussed doing the arias in Italian and the recitative in English but this seemed an awkward compromise. The fact that we are putting on an opera written in Italian by a Viennese composer, performed in English to an audience who are mainly French - adds a little to the madness of the whole enterprise.

But then I hear Donna's lovely clear soprano voice replying to Dan: 'What are you measuring, my darling?' And I realise it really doesn't matter. One of the advantages of opera is that it crosses international borders effortlessly. We once heard a performance of the Barber of Seville in Moscow. The synopsis in our programme was in Russian. Not knowing the opera, I took the Count in his disguises to be three different people. But who cares - it was a magical evening anyway.

The following morning Fred is setting Act Two. Fred and Kate keep turning up at the kitchen door with requests.

'Would it be all right if we took the chaise-longue from the Music Room?'

'Go ahead, it's fine.'
'Have you got a hammer?'
'Have you got a mandolin?'
'No, but I've got an old guitar.'
'Have you got a fan?'
'Have you got a screen?'
'Have you got a petticoat?'
'Have you got a bell?'

The requests come thick and fast and I can hear Kate going 'dot-and-carry-one' up and down the stairs. I hope she isn't overdoing it. I'm busy searching for props upstairs when I realise the cast are actually rehearsing IN the sitting room.

I come down and stand in the doorway. This year Donna is playing Susanna, while the older and more experienced Helen, is playing the Countess. Donna is perched on the chaise-longue. Fred is busy showing her how to hold the guitar and pick on it like a mandolin. When he straightens up, I catch his eye.

'But this room is perfect for the Countess's bedroom,' he protests.
'And where is the audience going to be?'
'They can watch though the windows and doorways.'
'On foot?'
'Well, Act Two isn't that long.'
'It's far too long for the audience to stand. Half of them won't even get a decent view.'

I go on a search for Peter to back me up but he's gone to the village to stock up for lunch. Peter had become chief shopper and lunch maker. His work on the allotment is paying dividends. Lettuce, tomatoes, cucumbers, French beans, courgettes and pumpkins are giving us bumper crops because of the storms. He makes massive salads for lunch in a couple of washbowls. I count myself lucky that he's so obsessed by food, I can delegate lunch-making to him. I avoid Fred's eye during lunch and take Jane aside.

'Don't worry, leave it to me,' she says. 'I'll make Fred see sense.'

That afternoon Fred 'seeing sense' involves most of the furniture from the sitting room being relocated to the terrace. I watch my precious bergère suite being carried out. I even catch Kate taking down the curtains and re-hanging them outside the windows. The window through which Cherubino will jump will mean Kitty will actually arrive in the kitchen.

'What happens if it rains?' I whisper to Peter.

'Well, at least we won't have the audience in the flowerbed.'

But it doesn't look as if it's going to rain. In fact it's incredibly hot. I check the thermometer as it rises to the mid '30's. I ransack all the cupboards for sun hats. Sun umbrellas are brought out to shield the piano and the cast all slather themselves in sun oil. We have the rare treat of seeing Mozart sung in swimwear.

The swimming pool has come into its own. The cast have found our old badminton net and erected it mid-way across the pool. Between rehearsals energetic games of water polo take place. In a rare moment of silence I go down to the pool to check that nobody is getting sunburnt and find a group of them up to their necks in water testing each other on their lines. I'm impressed as ever by the singers' dedication. In this kind of weather our kids would be stretched out plugged into their i-pods, lost to the world.

By Thursday Fred seems to be worryingly behind in his rehearsal schedule. I go to the hall to check the notice board and find he's not rehearsing Act Four until the evening. Friday will be devoted to cleaning up rough bits and a complete dress rehearsal will take place in the evening, timed to fit with the actual performance the following day. So he only has Thursday evening for the last act.

Pam is running round with a tape measure round her neck and a mouthful of pins. Last minute adjustments to the costumes mean she's chained to the sewing machine. The iron is on twelve hours a day. I cast a discerning eye over the 'Twenties dresses Fred's friends have made. They are pretty basic, I'm starting to think that Pam and I could have done better. The boys are OK. They're in pretty standard blazers and dinner jackets. There's not a lot left to do for them apart for making Antonio - the gardener's – costume. Pam has made some sacking 'ligers' – string-thingees that tie around the lower legs – and is cutting an apron out of an old bit of leather that covered a chair in a previous life.

I catch Jane and air my worries about timing. 'It'll be fine,' she says. 'Fred's such a night owl. He'll probably have us rehearsing till breakfast.'

That evening I can see the logic in Fred's decision. He's set Act Three in the box hedges at the front of the house. These rather wild bushes must once have been miniature hedges, planted in the pattern of a French formal garden. Over a century or more, left to their own devices, they've grown to a height of over two metres. I've often stared down at them from the attic trying to work out what sort of pattern they might have formed - most probably a rough sort of fleur-de-lys. We've been gradually pruning away, trying to get them back into some sort of order. So far we've achieved a number of tall hedges with a kind of arched arbour in between. This arrangement allows for multiple entrances and exits - just right for the opera's final act when the Count thinks he's having an illicit liaison with Susanna, but gets completely duped in the process and ends up mistakenly making love to his own wife. The arbour is the perfect setting for high jinx in the dark and romantic liaisons in shady corners.

By mid afternoon Kate and I are fixing up lights to be trained down from the front bedroom windows. We're tangled in metres of extension cables and nobody's going to have a bedside light tonight. We won't know what the whole thing will look like until the sun goes down.

We have an early supper and Peter, Pam and I finish the washing up listening to strains of Act Four coming from the garden. Nic is only just coping with the part of Don Basilio, he's really a music theatre singer and hasn't had the classical training of the others. Sadly Barbarina's lovely aria, when she's looking for the pin, has been cut as we're one soprano short. I go up and check from an upper window to see how the lighting is working. It's way too bright, the cast is either in glaring spotlight or inky shadow. We don't have any gels and there's no way we're going to source these locally. I make a note to go to the DIY shop tomorrow and get lower voltage bulbs.

By eleven they are about half way through the act. Pam heads for home and Peter and I go up to bed. Tomorrow is going to be a pretty heavy day. Pam and I are going to be standing by for fittings and alterations, if needed, to the costumes. And I want to get the house looking at its best for Saturday night.

Peter and I lie in bed in the warm night with the windows thrown open hearing the voices floating up to us. It's impossible to sleep and it would be a crime anyway, with such music to listen to. Eventually Fred gets to the final quartet – I think Mozart's favourite was actually in Don Giovanni – but this one must have come close. We fall asleep to its final magical chords.

Saturday dawns strangely misty. Peter posts a worrying forecast up on the notice board. Storms are due to come over from the West, it's not entirely clear when they will strike. Everyone is subdued at breakfast and one by one people get up from the table and check the clouds massing overhead. By ten a brisk wind has come up.

'It's going to be far too cold to eat outside,' I say.

'Even in the courtyard?'

'If the audience eats inside, we can probably perform the opera outside. Let's just hope everyone brings wraps and things.'

Peter is given the job of telling Fred that we may have to do the whole opera in the attic.

The decision to feed a hundred people inside the house means a massive job in furniture moving. Leo and boyfriend Baz have turned up and Claudia has one of her Parisians in tow. The two boys and members of the cast set to carrying furniture from the house into the barn to make space for the tables inside.

Once this is done, Fred takes the cast upstairs to reset Acts Two and Three. Cherubino's jump through the window is problematic as Kitty will actually be three storeys up. Kate and one of the boys are given the task of rigging up a make-shift window. They are asking Peter to help. Fat chance. DIY isn't exactly Peter's forte.

It has gone into family lore that once historically he was trying to force a light fitting to stay on the wall:

Peter (to me between gritted teeth) 'Where's the screwdriver?'
Me: 'In the tool shed.'

79

Pause

Peter: 'Where's the tool shed?'

After we've all had lunch I set to cooking the hundred chicken breasts for the lemon chicken. The meal is going to be a lot simpler this year. Last year seeing the French piling their plates with a horrible cocktail of dishes was a salutary lesson. This year there'll be no choice. It's a slice of fish paté as starter (bought from the supermarket), then chicken in a lemon sauce (served chilled), potato salad, green salad and apricot tarts from the patisserie to follow. But the chicken has to be cooked - all hundred and ten breasts. The kitchen already feels like a furnace as Peter is boiling the hundreds of new potatoes for the salad. But outside the temperature has dropped to the mid-twenties. At around three the rain sets in.

Fred comes down to us looking really depressed. Peter goes up to his computer and checks the weather forecast for the umpteenth time. He comes back with the good news that the storm should be over by nine. With any luck we can still play the final act in the shrubbery.

By four that afternoon the chicken is cooked but I'm so hot from the cooking that I go for a swim in the rain. Thunder rumbles in the distance and I wonder if swimming pools can be struck by lightening. I get out to be on the safe side. There are still three hours to go before the performance is due to start. I send up a silent prayer to the rain gods begging them to head off East. There's still a chance it could all clear up by seven.

The cast has had the afternoon off. A few are playing cards on the kitchen table. I find Donna, worryingly, lying on her bedroom floor with her feet up on a cushion.

'Are you OK?'

'I think I've done something to my back.'

'How?'

'When Fred caught me in the 'fainting' bit, I must have twisted something.'

I hurry downstairs and find Kate. She's professional and efficient. She quietly examines Donna and then gently starts massaging her back. I leave her to it.

Ten minutes or so later she comes downstairs looking worried.

'Is she all right?'

'I'm not sure. I've given her some anti-inflammatories and I've left her to rest.'

The others have stopped their card game. There's a tense silence. Our planning doesn't allow for understudies. If Donna can't sing, we have no Susanna. Without Susanna we have no Marriage of Figaro.

'I'll go up and see her,' says Fred. He comes down a few minutes later.

'She insists she'll be all right by this evening.'

'What do you think?' I ask Kate.

'We'll have to see when the time comes.'

In the meantime, we still have to prepare for a hundred guests. Everyone has to chip in. Nic has volunteered to help Peter. Baz and Claudia lay the tables - her current Parisian is busy smoking somewhere under a tree in the garden. Leo has been given the job of putting new candles in the candlesticks. Marjorie is folding programmes and Pam is still tied up at the sewing machine dealing with a frayed hem. From above I can hear Helen going through her arpeggios again.

Jane comes by with a frown. 'If she goes on like that, she's going to give herself a sore throat.' There's a little friction I've noticed between the sopranos, not exactly professional jealousy but certainly some competitiveness.

At around five it's still raining. M. Aubertin has turned up in a sou'wester and gumboots. He puts on his official P armband and sets off to the orchard to tie road-menders red and white striped tape round the trees to create alleyways. We just pray the cars don't get bogged down in mud. By five-thirty everyone has disappeared to dress. All the hot taps in all the bathrooms go on in unison as people take showers.

I go and check on Donna. She's up and dressing although she still looks pale.

'Are you sure you're going to be all right?'

'I'm fine, honestly.'

'We can still cancel you know. We can just give them dinner.'

'Or I could lie down and sing from the wings.'

'Yes.'

'No. I'm dosed up with pain-killers. I'll be all right.'

In fact, Donna sang Susanna without giving the slightest indication of the pain she was suffering. It was only later, when they had a second performance in England, that she had to drop out and another girl took her part. It took several months for her back to get better. This was one more example of the singers' total commitment. Quite humbling really.

So it seemed we had a performance. Our next problem was the weather. The wind had got up and the temperature was dipping even further. Weather like this didn't seem possible in August.

I got down to the kitchen and found that Jacqueline and two of her sisters had arrived. They'd taken charge of the kitchen and suddenly everything was falling into place. The washing up was done and stacked and they were swabbing down the surfaces.

Jacqueline has designated herself chief of the catering corps and is demanding jugs for water, trays for glasses, more bottle openers, sets of salad servers and baskets for bread - all the things I've overlooked. I obediently rush around finding the things that are missing.

'And what's happened to the hot water?' she says accusingly, holding her hand under the tap. The hot water tap is running cold. I explain about the showers and she gives a dismissive sniff and puts some saucepans of water on the stove to heat.

Peter arrives, speech in hand, trying to fix his bow tie. It's still raining and the decision has been made to do the first three acts in the attic. The cast are frantically busy carrying props, furniture and the piano upstairs. Baz and the Parisian, who actually pauses from smoking long enough to help, are carrying plastic chairs, four at a time up the winding staircase for the audience.

Fred arrives downstairs, looking splendid, dressed as the Count in a dinner jacket.

'Where are the audience having the welcome drinks?' he asks.

'In the sitting room and dining room.'

These are both choc-a-bloc with tables laid for dinner. I suppose they'll just have to find a way to fit in in-between.

'Can you get as many as possible in the hall?'

'Sure. Why?'

'Not telling.' He sweeps up the stairs to the attic.

The rain actually eases off as the audience arrives. Briefly, we step outside, but just as Peter is about to start his speech the clouds open and the rain pelts down again. There's a bit of a scramble as we all crowd into the hallway.

Peter's waving his speech in the air and there's a lot of shushing for silence. Nobody wants to miss this gem of perfectly pronounced French. He spoils it by adding a few impromptu bits of his own about the 'Meteo' and 'chats et chiens' a piece of franglais which totally passes the French by. However they give him enthusiastic applause. Then I'm dismayed to see the cast marching down from the attic. For a few ghastly mini-seconds that feel like an eternity, I try to fathom out what's gone wrong: The roof has leaked on to the piano and fused it? Donna's passed out? The floor has collapsed?

They position themselves on the staircase. They look reassuringly composed - what's Fred up to? I glance around for the piano. It's nowhere to be seen. As I turn back, the cast begins to sing. Roland has re-written Figaro's famous overture in his own version for voices. It's a hilarious 'a capella' arrangement full of trills and pom-poms.

Suddenly the weather doesn't matter. The audience roars with laughter and applauds. The cast turn heel and run up the stairs, the audience follows, everyone chattering at once. The opera has begun, full of fun as Figaro should be. And even if it is in the attic and the music is accompanied by the unorthodox addition of rain pelting on tiles above our heads, no-one cares.

The First Act has been planned for the attic anyway. Donna is a delight as the young bride Susanna. What a change from last year. The sixteen-year-old, who could hardly raise her eyes to the audience, has metamorphosed into a playful seventeen-year-old. Bad back seemingly forgotten, she's acting the part with flair and a rare talent for comedy. And that voice of hers has matured in tone and grown in volume.

Fred makes a wonderful Count, in turns puffed up with self-importance and then deflated. I worry slightly for the stability of our antique chair as he and Cherubino take turns in hiding in it. Susanna's 'fainting' is more of a fit of the vapours – I'm relieved to see Donna's taking care.

Act Two arrives and there's a lot of shuffling of furniture as my chaise-longue appears out of the shadows. Somehow it has made it upstairs, god knows how they got it round the corners. Helen, thankfully hasn't practised herself hoarse, she's a commendably tragic Countess and a lovely foil for Fred's irascible Count. As Fred frets and storms around the stage, getting himself more tightly entangled in the opera's plot, somehow I can't help being reminded of Peter in one of his Basil Fawlty moods – maybe Fred's been studying him. The Count exits, taking the Countess with him, to find a suitable implement to force open the cupboard door behind which he expects to find his wife's lover.

The scene progresses, the make-shift window doesn't fall to pieces as Kitty climbs out through. I'm starting to relax – it's all going smoothly – when Fred storms back in, wild with jealousy intent on battering the door open, armed with *a sink plunger*. This brings the house down. It's so like Peter in one of his blind and fruitless rages. I learned later that this wasn't an intentional bit of business. In the rush to take everything upstairs, Kate had forgotten the hammer and Fred grabbed the first thing he could lay his hands on.

When we reach the dinner interval, it's clear that the decision to eat inside has been the right one. It's really cold now and the boiler has gone strangely silent. I slip out to the boiler room to see what has happened and find a red warning light I've never seen before winking at me. It seems the boiler has taken umbrage at the volume of hot water demanded of it and has turned itself off. Central heating simply isn't an option. I go back into the diners, wishing I'd planned a hot meal instead of a cold one. But bottles are being uncorked and the audience is getting into the swing of things.

I settle into my seat and make the best of it. We've separated all the couples and I can see Peter deep into pretending to listen to the fellow opposite him who is telling him in fast and unintelligible French about some recent governmental scandal. The potato salads are already on the tables and the French have decided these are a first course. They've finished them and wiped their plates clean with bread by the time the lemon chicken arrives. But no worries, this goes down a treat with plenty more bread dipped in the sauce. The embarrassingly simple food is disappearing fast, in fact they seem perfectly happy with it.

Peter takes furtive trips outside to check the weather. Our eyes meet, he shakes his head. It seems that Act Four will have to be played upstairs as well. Fred is going to be devastated, he'd set his heart on having it in the box walk. But the rain has truly set in for the night.

My meal has been constantly interrupted by Kate and M. Aubertin who keep sidling up to me with requests for clippers, saws and hammers, ropes, wire and a staple gun. I wonder what the hell is going on. Something must have collapsed in the attic. I should never have trusted that odd-job man with the floor.

Kate comes and whispers in my ear: Can I keep the audience downstairs a bit longer? She'll ring the bell when they're ready to start. This is no problem, the audience is well into catching up on another year's gossip. We'll be lucky if we can make the bell heard over the din.

The bell rings and Kate gives me the 'all clear'. I lead the way up the winding stairs. In the attic doorway I stop and catch my breath. They've transformed it into a garden. Huge branches hang down from the beams. A statue from the terrace is wound with ivy. Everything glitters with raindrops in the half light. I can see M.Aubertin standing in the wings looking very pleased with himself.

I watch the final act in a sort of haze. My dream of performing Figaro has come to pass. But it has all passed so fast. As the last melting chords of the final quartet fade away. I want to catch this moment and record it in my head, to play back over and over again.

The French are good at applause. Like their speeches, it goes on far longer than in England. Really enthusiastic applause ends in slow clapping, the first time I heard it I'd interpreted it as disapproval. But the cast is reassembling. They're going to give an encore. Oddly Nic has been pushed to centre stage. And then he sings the first notes of Britney Spears' "Hit me Baby one more time." The rest of the cast come in with the backing track. There are hisses like drum snags and a ridiculous parody of other instruments. Nic is brilliant as the lead vocalist. There's laughter, more applause, more demands for encores. I wonder if we're ever going to get the audience to leave.

Peter jumps up with bottles of champagne for the cast and delivers a rather drunken speech in English which hopefully no-one understands. And then suddenly it is all over.

The tail-lights of the last car wind out through the orchard. Peter and I stand and watch. Miraculously the rain has ceased, the clouds blown away and the sky is set with a million stars.

'It's really sad that it's over.' I say.

Him: 'Umm'

Me: 'I mean it was a pity we couldn't do it outside like we planned. But it was OK wasn't it?'

Him: 'Umm.'

Me: 'You're very quiet.'

Him: 'I've been thinking.'

Me: 'Umm?'

Him: 'About next year.'

Me: 'Next year?'

'How about Don Giovanni?'

I knew there had to be a reason I married this man.

With cruel irony the next day dawns bright and clear. It's going to be hot. I come downstairs to find the house looks as if a bomb has hit it. No, that's not quite right, there are empty bottles everywhere. The house actually looks as if a load of drunken, marauders have invaded and tried to turn the place into a rather decadent squat. There are no singers to be seen but there are signs of their partying in the oddest places. I find a pair of bathing trunks in the dishwasher.

'Must have mistaken it for a washing machine.' Pam's standing over me with a tray loaded with glasses. She's been in the house since dawn and has already done quite an impressive tidy up. She's looking remarkably fresh for someone who tried to drink the place dry last night. My head is pounding and I feel as if someone has taken out my eyeballs and put them back in the wrong way round.

'I need coffee,' I groan and try to locate an unencumbered surface on which to make it. We have coffee and toast remnants of last night's bread, and plaster them with honey.

'Fred's already up,' says Pam.
'He can't be.'
'He's outside in the park, smoking.'

I crane out through the French windows and catch sight of a wisp of smoke coming from the far end of the lawn.

'He's really depressed,' says Pam.
'About not doing Figaro outside?'
'No, about life in general.'

This is news to me. Fred is always so full of fun. He has such a brilliant sense of humour. I'd never seen his darker side.

Pam nods. 'I was talking to him last night. He's in a bad way.'

'Maybe he should lose weight,' I say irrelevantly, licking honey off my fingers.

'He needs a sense of direction. He doesn't know what to do with his life.'

'But he's brilliant. Look at how he re-worked the libretto. He's a great director. And singer.'

'He wants to be an actor.'

'I see.' I wonder how many parts there can be for a roly-poly person the size of Fred.

'I think I know of something that might cheer him up,' I take a tray with coffee and a plate of toast and Nutella out to the orchard.

'Hi Fred, I want to show you something.'

Fred gets to his feet. He does look pretty depressed. His eyes are red round the rims.

I lead him over to the pond. It's not very big or very deep but we've added a little curved bridge to give a touch of 'Monet' to it – there were meant to be water lilies too but every time we planted them the ducks ate them.

'Wouldn't this be just the thing for Don Giovanni? You know the moment when those three Dons in masks arrive for Don Giovanni's ball – they could stand on the bridge.'

Fred stares at me. 'You don't mean it?'

'Yes. Peter's idea. Don Giovanni. Next year.'

Fred truly has tears in his eyes now. 'But I thought you just wanted to do 'Figaro' and that would be it.'

'Let's just say you talked – no sang – us into it.'

Fred hugs me.

'So you'll do it? I mean, hopefully we could actually perform outside, next time.'

'You're sure you wouldn't prefer The Magic Flute?'

Here we go again!

Later that day the cast get up in various states of hangover. Donna is positively catatonic, she seems to have lost the ability to speak but her back seems better. I feel a little anxious for the Terray's performance - which is due to take place that evening – will she be able to sing?

Peter and I make a vast brunch: sausages, bacon, eggs, tomatoes, baked beans and fried potatoes plus piles of toast and croissants all washed down with pots of tea. Marjorie arrives to join us. This is the first English breakfast she's had in months – she puts away a mammoth portion for someone her age – making up for lost time no doubt.

As they eat, the singers gradually come back to life. All that is, apart from Donna, who is still staring fixedly at the wall. She has gone a very strange colour. At around midday Leo, Claudia, Baz and the Parisian arrive downstairs, register shock at the state of the house and take themselves off for a civilised lunch in a neighbouring chateau hotel.

Typical!

That afternoon there's a brocante (street market) in the neighbouring village. The entire cast, apart from Donna, want to go. We dose Donna with paracetemol and CocaCola and send her back to bed. The rest of the cast leave with our cars. Peter retires for a siesta and Pam and I start to clear the tables from the night before. The dishwasher has already done three loads and the two washing machines have been on non-stop. (Yes, two – I was prepared). The boiler seems to have recovered from its fit of the sulks, I pressed the red button and was rewarded by a familiar roar.

'So how did you cheer Fred up?' Pam asks.

'I told him we want to do Don Giovanni next year.'

She stares at me. 'You can't be serious.'

'No?'

'Aren't you meant to be getting back to work? That book you've got a deadline for?'

'It's ages till next summer.'

'Can you afford it?'

'We can if we cut some corners. And if I get that advance.'

I'd been offered a rather generous advance by Bloomsbury – the publishers of Harry Potter – who, probably due to H.P. must have been feeling pretty flush.

'You better get on with that book then.'

'Yeah well, maybe we ought to clear up first.'

That year clearing up took ages. I have since learned a few tricks:

How to get red wine out of linen: Soak it in a cold washing soda solution and then put it through a hot wash.

How to get candle-wax off fabric: Cover it with brown paper and iron through it. The paper soaks up the wax.

How to get candlewax off candlesticks: Put them in the deep freeze then chip it off.

How to press twelve linen tablecloths in one go: Dry them on the line, then carefully fold them. Pile them one on top of each other then put a board on top and weight it with the heaviest thing you can find. Buckets of water work a treat.

Oh and I've found a brilliant oven cleaner. 'What's it called?' asks Pam.

'Jacqueline'.

The cast were late back and dashed up to their rooms to prepare for the Terrays. We drove to their chateau in convoy. Peter and I were guests this time and were looking forward to enjoying their performance without feeling stressed. But what with the brocante and everything we arrived a little late. The Terrays had around sixty guests waiting for us on the lawn in front of the chateau. The cast got the piano linked up at breakneck speed and Roland came out to the front holding up a hand for silence. He then gave a speech, off the cuff, in immaculate French. I exchanged glances with Peter. He's kept that one to himself. We were constantly being surprised by Roland's many talents.

We'd promised the Terrays arias and ensembles from Figaro but the cast had a few ideas of their own. Kate, Jane and Helen sang 'I feel pretty,' from West Side Story. Fred did a number from Sondheim's Sweeney Todd in which he'd performed the Barber the year before with Bedfordshire Youth Opera. But the item that earned the most applause was the whole troupe backing Nic with their 'a capella' version of "Hit me Baby one more time."

We returned home thinking that was it for another year. But the cast insisted we join them in the courtyard for a glass of champagne before going to bed. When all our glasses were filled they got in a huddle and sang 'Teddy Bear's Picnic' for Peter. Then Jane sashayed out on her high heels and presented us with a lovely antique brass handbell they'd bought at the brocante as a thank you present.

A brass bell that has called many singers to the table since and also featured in several operas.

Chapter Ten

Another winter passes. The magical strains of Figaro that seemed to linger in ghostly echoes around the house have faded. I can just catch a bat-squeak of them when I go up to the attic where the makeshift 'window' Cherubino climbed through is still leaning against the wall.

Christmas comes and among my gifts Peter gives me a DVD of Don Giovanni. It's a strange Christmas. Both Leo and Claudia are 'single' again. Claudia has broken up with her latest Parisian, who I've secretly named 'Beastly Julien'. Leo has ended her six-year relationship with childhood sweetheart Baz. I'm sad because we're fond of him.

We've invited a couple of friends from England, whose son and daughter who are 36 and 32 respectively are also on their own. Pam's mother, daughter, son in law and children, who are over from the UK, are invited for lunch. You could hardly find a more ill-assorted table ranging from Marjorie at ninety-four down to Pam's smallest grandchild aged three – dressed as a fairy princess complete with wings.

Marjorie's feeling the cold so in January I take her to Australia to visit my sister Juliet. The minute I climb off the plane in Perth I feel that I'm coming back to life with an adrenalin rush of summer light and heat. Communication with Peter is by email. There's a hiatus over a day or so, he doesn't answer my mails. It's probably something to do with our modem, it's sensitive to fluctuations. I wonder if he'll manage to call France Telecom and get them to sort it out. That night I lie awake praying that he hasn't fallen downstairs or cut his leg off with the chainsaw or something. The following day I'm relieved to find an email from him headed: 'Still alive – *just.*'

Apparently the day before he went into an upstairs bathroom for reasons we don't need to go into and, as he closed the door, the handle came off in his hand. Not the handle with the long thingee on it, but the other one. (N.B. if you ever fit a door handle, make sure the side with the long thingee is on the inside – not as M. Sandrin had done – the other way round.) The door was very solid. He gave it a little shake. It was well and truly closed. He went to the window and looked out. There was a sheer drop of twenty or so metres below. He saw a tractor passing in the lane and opened the window and shouted – unheard. He then sat down on the closed loo-lid and thought about his predicament. You don't normally take a mobile phone into the bathroom with you and he hadn't. No-one was going to visit. No-one was likely to phone apart from me, and that might not be for days and I would just think he was out shopping or something. He wasn't going to die of thirst, but he was going to get pretty hungry. He opened the window again and did a bit more fruitless shouting. It would get cold at night too because, as an economy measure, I'd programmed the heating to go off at night. There were only two towels to wrap himself in - two towels that - at a stretch - tied together would only reach a metre or so below the window (he'd thought of that one). The fact that I was callously sunning myself in Australia while he was being reduced to a starving shivering skeleton in an icy bathroom didn't help.

Nearly a day later, with only a couple of glasses of tap water for sustenance, Peter had an uncharacteristically practical thought. He'd brought his sponge bag into the bathroom with him, because that morning he'd discovered one of those annoying white hairs growing vertically out of the top of his nose. (I call them 'unicorns' and I'm very particular about their removal). He kept a pair of tweezers in his sponge-bag for this purpose.

Very, very carefully, so as not to dislodge the long thingee in the lock, he eased the tweezers in and grasped it. It was slippery and the tweezers weren't really strong enough but when he twisted them, it turned. The door opened. He walked out a free man. So simple. Now why hadn't he thought of that hours before?

But back to the opera. Once safely back at his desk, Peter was in touch with Jane. She was starting to cast Don Giovanni. As ever the women were not a problem, Donna would play Donna Anna, and Helen would play Donna Elvira while Jane would play the peasant girl, Zerlina. Fred could play the Commendatore but they needed two really good male singers for the Don and Leporello.

We're still dining out on Peter's bathroom predicament when he emails with the good news that they've found an excellent Don Giovanni: Philip Spendley – he's a bit older than the others. Jane enthuses about his voice. What about Leporello? I email back, trying to sound involved. In fact, Opera Loki seems a very long way away, like a dream of something that never happened. It's hard to believe that in a few months we'll be running a house full of singers again.

In the mornings I bash away on Juliet's computer. I have a deadline to meet for Bloomsbury – we need the money to fund this year's performance. Juliet paints in her studio, she has an exhibition coming up in the Autumn and is a few paintings short. Over lunch we exchange commiserations about how badly our work is going. In the afternoons we take Marjorie out for strawberry teas and visits to wineries, cider makers, and potters - anything fairly sedentary that you can do with a ninety four year old.

We leave for France as autumn arrives in Western Australia. It has actually rained. When we arrive back home, we find spring has arrived. The switch of seasons has got Marjorie confused, she's just had summer and now it's happening all over again.

Peter is delighted to have us back – quite the perfect husband for a while. I get down to the backlog of washing, defrosting the fridge in which the ice-box door has frozen closed, sorting out the frying pan with the handle selotaped on because the screw has come loose. I quietly put away the row of knives that he has out on the worktop in order of size and sharpness, the toppling pile of books and newspapers he is currently reading and the seven pairs of his shoes gathering dust by our bedside.

As the days grow longer we are getting excited about this year's opera. M. Aubertin has been hard at work in the garden. He's cleared a path we didn't even know existed down the side of the meadows. It must once have been the driveway to the house. Two hundred or so years ago it was planted with an avenue of trees. Some are missing now and others lean at crazy angles but they form a towering canopy with a narrow shaded tunnel beneath – this becomes my favourite daily walk. The debris from his handiwork has been piled into a six metre high bonfire waiting for a long enough dry period to burn.

We have three dry days in succession and we take basket-loads of old manuscripts and documents out to the bonfire.
M. Aubertin has doused the pile with a can of old engine oil. Peter

throws in a match and we stand well back. The fire goes up with an impressive 'FWOOOMPH'. We can see the house through the flames, with the tower rising above, clear of the smoke. It looks weirdly as if the whole house is on fire. I rush inside for my camera. Peter grudgingly agrees that my 'brilliant' photo can be used for the cover of the Don Giovanni programme.

Pam and I are starting to worry about the costumes. It seems logical to set the opera traditionally in the 18th Century, since that is also the period of the house - but we don't think Fred's 'friends' are up to making 18th Century costumes. Jane looks into hiring the costumes in London - we're going to need them for at least a week and we also have the problem of getting them to France. After the SNCF disaster of the previous year, Peter has decided to fly the cast to Clermont Ferrand. Bulky 18th Century costumes are going to add expensive excess baggage. Jane comes back with an estimate. It's way over our budget. A week or so later she emails to say that the Costume Department of the London Coliseum is having a sale. She manages to secure a peasant outfit that will do for Zerlina but their other 18th C costumes are far too pricey.

In June Peter has to go off on another of his international trips. Pam and I are invited to lunch by our neighbours, the Civreis, whose christian names are conveniently easy to remember - François and Françoise. Françoise is the kind person who brought armfuls of flowers for last year's opera. François is always ready to lend his ancient Landrover which has a tow-bar, when we need it for heavy jobs. They live in a nearby hunting lodge that dates back to the 15th Century and belonged to the same family as our house. I've always longed to see inside this house as an idea is forming in my mind of a book I want to write about the history of La Gozinière. I'm not disappointed. La Trolière has conical towers of warm russet tiles and is surrounded by a moat. It's going to be an informal lunch, served in the kitchen, which is an extra treat because the kitchen is in the base of one of the towers. The grill is over an open fire and Francoise is cooking us steaks in much the same way as they would have been cooked centuries ago.

Over lunch the subject of the costumes come up. 'But why don't you try Chez Jeanne?' asks Françoise.

It seems there's a costume hire shop in the nearby town of Montluçon. I was soon to learn that the French love nothing better than to dress up or to be 'deguisé' as they put it. They leap at any chance to strip off their togs and get dolled up, the more extravagant the theme the better. In France you find dress hire shops in the most unexpected places.

The following Tuesday (on Monday everything is closed – the French need a decent three-day weekend) Pam and I drove to Montluçon.

We find 'Chez Jeanne' tucked away between a flower shop and a gift shop in the old town. But it's closed. We peer through the window. Tantalizingly, glimpses of gold embroidery and lacy sleeves can be seen in the gloom. Maybe we're too early, it's two thirty (the French need a proper two-hour lunch hour – or even maybe three-hour to include a coffee and digest their lunch). We go for a walk round the old town. We arrive back at ten past three 'Chez Jeanne' is still closed. Maybe it's closed for good.

Pam is not to be put off. She walks over to a nearby café and demands whether anyone knows where Jeanne is. Someone stubs out a fag, rises wearily from a table and finds a mobile in a drawer. After a minute or so, a woman of around fifty with flaming red hair, dressed suitably flamboyantly, strides down the street. 'Jeanne' draws a huge key out of an inside pocket and opens up the shop.

It's a treasure trove. Pam and I give little squeals of delight as we find buckskin breeches and thigh-high boots for the Don.

There are several 18th Century dresses. We have a pretty good idea of the girls' sizes and I try on a few. Conveniently, they lace up at the back which allows a certain leeway for waists and boobs – especially boobs – because although pretty slim - most of the girls are well endowed in that department. I'm starting to think, it must have some effect on a soprano's tone or pitch or whatever.

We unearth an armful of lacy shirts and petticoats and a couple of cloaks. We are so excited by our finds that I'm not totting up the cost of it all. Before long we have put a pile of clothes to one side and I watch anxiously as Jeanne goes through them noting down the prices.

'How long will you need them?' she asks.

I say that if we can have them on the Wednesday before the performance we can return them on the Monday.

'I'm closed on Monday so we won't count that,' she says. Then she comes out with a figure I've only dreamed of.

'Are you sure?'

'Well, I could make a reduction since you're taking so many items.' She's misunderstood my amazement. 'And after all it is for a theatrical production,' she adds with a smile. 'I adore the theatre.'

We drive home hardly able to believe our luck. I ring Fred. He's nowhere near as thrilled as we are. It seems his 'friends' are going to be very disappointed not to get the job. It dawns on me at this point that suddenly the costumes have become our responsibility. I just hope we're doing the right thing.

It's now May and the weather is miserable. Pam and I watch my Don Giovanni DVD as we sew together. She's teaching me how to do upholstery – a necessary skill as half the furniture I've bought second hand is either worn on the armrests or sagging at the bottom. The DVD has Kiri Te Kanawa as Donna Anna and Placido Domingo as Don Giovanni. It's lavishly set in Vicenza with La Rotonde as the Don's cushy pad. We are positively drooling over the opulence of the costumes and beauty of the setting and all that southern sunshine. Roll on summer. We make long lists of the costumes required.

It seems we have nothing to turn the flesh and blood Commendatore (Fred) into a stone statue. We're also going to need masks and 18th Century hats. I ring another close friend, Roselyne. She's a painter and runs courses at our local art school. One of them is mask-making, Pam and I go down to the art school to see if any of these will do. She has fabulous hand-made masks but unfortunately they're all full-face, so no good for our singers. She comes up with a solution for the hats however. Her husband is a hatter. Serendipity again! His family have been hat makers for generations. They actually made hats for kings and heads of state. He has a wonderful atelier equipped with traditional wooden head-blocks and the steaming equipment for making felt hats. Currently he's working flat out on an order for Hermès but, when he has the time, he has a load of thick black felt he very kindly says is going begging. He offers to make us three hats as a gift.

Peter's busy on the guest list. This year Charles Osborne, Mozart expert and critic whose synopses have been invaluable has promised to come with his boyfriend – my great friend, Ken. It's more than a little scary, Charles has been scathing about some of Maria Callas' performances! Peter's getting the Don Giovanni synopsis translated into French. Emails are going back and forth via Jane about cuts and changes Fred's making to the libretto. One in particular is a pity, Don Ottavio's aria has been cut – Nic's going to play Ottavio and this aria is just too difficult for him.

There will be another new member of the audience, Connie, Pam's mother, who came at Christmas. At 88 she's a mere spring chicken compared with Marjorie. I'm hoping she'll enjoy it. We took her to a concert of a Russian Orthodox choir last year and as we came out, she was heard to say in her lovely Yorkshire accent: 'Yes, they were good. But if only they could've sung something I knew, like "Abide with Me".'

But members of the family will be fewer this year. Leo has made a life change after her break-up with Baz. She's chucked in the job she's had with the BBC and taken herself off to L.A. where she wants to develop a career as a film critic and life-style journalist. Claudia is coming to Gozinière with her replacement for 'Beastly Julien' - a four-legged one. She's always had a cat and the last one, Sid Vicious (by name and nature), turned out to be a disaster. He went missing the previous Autumn when she had a flat neighbouring the Bois de Vincennes. Tearful phone calls came to Gozinière as she tried to enlist everyone, from the local Postman to the entire staff of the Local Gendarmerie, to join in the search for him. I kept making comforting noises about Sid finding furry friends and living a happy feral life in the forest. All through the winter he was missing. Then one morning in spring, when it was warm enough to have the windows open, Claudia heard a plaintive meouw. A very scruffy and very skinny grey and white cat with markings very like Sid was standing outside. 'Sid' was washed and brushed and given a basket with a cashmere sweater to lie on and fed with fillet steak to strengthen him up. A few days later I happened to be coming up to Paris to help Claudia move to a new flat. (Hopefully, a cat-free flat.)

'You do think it's Sid, don't you?' said Claudia.

The cat in the basket leered at me with yellowed teeth. Who did he remind me of? Yes, Steptoe the elder.

'It can't be. This is an old cat - look at its claws. Sid was a kitten when you got him. He wouldn't be more than two by now.'

'But he spent the whole winter in the forest.'

'He's spent his whole life in the forest. He looks positively rabid.'

'Well, I think it's Sid.'

The argument went back and forth. The flat Claudia is moving to is in the centre of Paris, in the fashionable Left Bank quartier of St Germain des Prés. It's a small flat, without a garden, totally unsuitable for a cat. She wants me to take 'Sid' back to Gozinière. I'm objecting - heaven knows what will happen when he meets my two aristochats – they'll probably catch something from him.

'There's one way to solve this,' I said firmly. 'We'll take him to a vet. A vet will be able to tell his age.'

The vet was young and unfortunately very sympathetic. 'Sid' had disgraced himself on the way in the basket. As he cleaned up the mess, he listened to Claudia's sad tale.

'Well... of course it's always difficult to be sure of a cat's age...' he said, looking into Claudia's hopeful and dewy eyes.

'Rubbish,' I said. 'Look at its claws and its teeth.'

'How old did you say your cat was?'

'Two'/ 'Two and a half.' We say simultaneously.

'We-ell...'

'Sid' put on a purr and gazed up at the vet in a nasty sycophantic way. I'm steaming by this time. There is no way I'm going to take this vicious and incontinent imposter back to Gozinière.

'And what sex was your cat?' he asks turning to its rear end.

I hold my breath.

'A boy...'

'Ah Mademoiselle. I'm sorry, this cat is female.'
Phew!
We're back out in the waiting room with 'Sidonie' in the basket.
'Well, if it's not Sid, I don't want it,' says Claudia.
'But you were all over this cat a minute ago.'
'You can have it.'
'I don't want it even if it is Sid. It can go back in the forest.'

We both stare at Sidonie, who is looking hopefully through the bars of the basket. She tries to look appealing. (It helps if she keeps her mouth shut). She's not going to give up a life of cashmere and fillet steak that easily.

'She'll have to go to a refuge,' I say.
'But if they can't find a home, they you know – eutha-thingee - them,' says Claudia.

The young vet has overheard this. He pokes his head out from his consulting room door. 'As a matter of fact, I know of one refuge where they keep the cats if they can't find a home for them.'

He hands a slip of paper with the address to Claudia. There's no time to lose. Claudia is due to move to her new flat tomorrow.

'We'll drive there right away,' I say.

It's getting dark and it has started raining and the refuge is miles out in the suburbs. After an hour of negotiating dark ring roads with the windscreen wipers going like the clappers and a cat yowling in the back, we find the place.

There's a lovely lady who takes Sidonie in. We have a brief glimpse of a room full of cages. There's a strong smell of disinfectant. Claudia is about to change her mind when I hand the woman a generous donation to help with her refuge and frog-march her out.

'You will let me know what happens to…her. Won't you?' Claudia calls over her shoulder.

Amazingly, this story has a happy ending. A month later Claudia was sent a cutting from a newspaper. Sidonie was an old cat and she had Cat Aids (I was right about the age and the rabid bit) but an old couple wanted a cat that wouldn't outlive them and had given her a home.

After that, Peter and I made Claudia promise that as long as she lived in a flat, never, never to have another cat.

But we didn't say anything about a dog.

Enter Loki – Beastly Julien's four-legged replacement. (You see the digression did have a point).

Claudia bought Loki in one of those elegant pet shops on the Quai des Celestins. Her name, meaning 'God of Mischief', was apt. As a puppy she was a small white bundle of fluff. The mischief part was the fault of the vendors. They'd told Claudia, who had only ever had a cat before, that a dog could be trained to do its 'besoins' in a cat tray.

Complete rubbish of course and Loki was soon busy ruining the carpets in Claudia's new flat.

'Wouldn't you and Daddy like a dog at Gozinière?'

'No,' in unison.

Loki was a true Parisienne, all show and no content. She loved tripping along the pavements as if on high-heels, gazing from under her eyelashes at anyone who paused to admire her. On our occasional visits to Paris, Peter would reluctantly take her for a walk and come back telling us how friendly the people were in St Germain des Près, especially the blokes. But, as Peter said 'There was no way we were going to have Loki at Gozinière.'

Spring has turned to summer. The evenings are long and warm, we eat all our meals in the courtyard on a big marble table, another purchase from that salvage merchant in Mâcon - swallows fly overhead and Loki dozes underneath. Yes, of course we've taken her in. In fact, Pam has, but since she spends most of her time in our house anyway, Loki has become La Gozinière dog.

As the day of the singers' arrival approaches, Peter and M. Aubertin work hard on the allotment. M.Aubertin helps me spray the fruit trees and he comes out with a bucket and a stubby brush and paints all the trunks white. We are going to need all the fruit and veg. we can grow. The cast is up to twelve this year. We have an extra member of the troupe - a musical director, Ben Wiles, in addition to a new pianist Siobhan O'Higgins. Roland sadly can't make it as he's taken a rather prestigious job with a major global accountancy firm.

I tot up the numbers - with the cast, Marjorie, Pam, Connie and ourselves, we will be seventeen at every meal. Last year I squirreled away fruit in the deep freeze. There are red, black and white currants, three kinds of plums, blackberries, mulberries and raspberries, prepared apple for pies and bags of tiny poached peaches that I've discovered make the most impressive sorbet if you semi-defrost them, then mush them in the Magimix.

Pam and I make a list of our repertoire of dishes for mass feeding. Members of the cast are starting to request their favourites.

Chicken Curry – (pretty popular with everyone except Peter).

Pam's Moussaka (Jane's favourite).

Pam's Vegetable Lasagne (less popular with the boys who are all committed carnivores)

My Boeuf Bourguignon – (Kitty's favourite)

Our Cassoulet – (the jury's still out on this one)

My Potée d'Auvergnat (a succulent mixture of sausages, ham and Puy lentilles) Kate's favourite.

Anyone's Spaghetti Bolognese – (for the chaotic final night, quick and easy so we can fit in with the Dress Rehearsal.)

At last, the day of their arrival dawns. Peter drives off with a friend who has a seven-seater car and a trailer to pick up the cast. I make a last round of the rooms, counting the beds once again, making sure everyone has been assigned one and checking for loo rolls and soap in all the bathrooms.

The house is very quiet. I go up to the attic. The dormers have been thrown open to allow air to circulate, cooling the house. The weather is balmy and the garden is a deep luxurious green in the declining sunlight. It's so silent I can hear the sound of M.Aubertin raking on the allotment.

The 'Figaro' window is still leaning against the wall. Soon new voices are going to fill the house. New feet will be running up and down the stairs. Pots will be clattering in the kitchen and the sewing machine will be going non-stop. Marjorie still thinks we're mad to put on the opera. So-o much work! But if it's madness, I'm a happy lunatic. For me it's the best week of the year.

I hear the cars arriving on the gravel below and Loki barking fit to bust. I run downstairs, there are hugs from the cast we know and Loki is given the fuss she thinks she deserves. Jane introduces the new members of the cast – a tall, good-looking fellow, Phil Spendley, the tenor who is going to play Don Giovanni; and a baritone – Dan Grice, who will be singing the part of his servant - Leporello. There's Ben Wiles, the musical director, plus the new pianist Siobhan.

The best single rooms have been given to Siobhan, Helen, Donna, Phil and Dan since they will have to work the hardest. Fred is happy to share with Nic (apparently they're just good friends). Jane and Kate have offered to actually share a double bed. The others go into a kind of dormitory over Marjorie's apartment.

The new members of the cast wander round the house making flattering remarks about the size and beauty of it. I glow with pride. As far as I'm concerned it's the most beautiful house in France – in fact probably in the world (but maybe I'm biased). There are shouts and whoops coming from the garden. The old hands have reached the swimming pool and are cooling off after their journey.

Chapter Eleven

The following morning Fred and Jane collar me after breakfast. There's to be no messing about this year. We're all agreed, the opera is going to be a 'promenade' performance that will take place in several venues around the house and garden. The audience will have to carry their chairs round with them and the weather will have to behave. Fred is anxious to know where the dinner will be served and manages to persuade me out of my first choice – the courtyard – but to have it in front of the house on the lawn instead.

Having established this, he takes the cast into the courtyard to rehearse the first act. Pam and I take over what we call the TV room because it has our only TV and a cushy sofa to crash out on – and set up a sewing and costume base. I get a couple of the boys to bring the cheval mirror down from upstairs.

I've bought metres of dull grey material in the Marché St Pierre in Paris – there's a wonderful shop there called Reine where you get fabric for a few euros a metre. As the years have gone by, I've become a regular there. The problem in hand is to turn the Commendatore into a reasonably convincing stone statue. We're using an old cloak of Peter's as a model. Pam and I sellotape sheets of newspaper together and make a rough paper pattern for a cloak that reaches the ground. It has to be pretty large, since it's for Fred. We put our Don Giovanni DVD on the TV and start cutting out.

Kate comes in with various requests: Have we got a big basket? An old iron bucket for the well? Can we get some sheaves of wheat from the next door farmer? And where can she pick flowers for garlands? I leave Pam with the cloak problem and go searching for props. By the time I get back, the cloak is all cut out and she's run up the side seams. We need to catch Fred to try it on.

I've had the opera in mind all year. Our trips to Emmaüs have reaped their reward. There's nothing Pam and I like better than to drive off to Moulins, Montluçon or St Amand to see what has turned up during the week. 'You're going again?' Peter demands. 'It's for the opera,' is our excuse. I've stashed away numerous items that I've bought in case they might come in handy. Among them is a fantasy wine bucket made in the shape of the helmet from a suit of armour. Fred won't be able to wear it on his head but he can carry it under his arm, which should help make him look something like a military statue. When Fred tries the cloak on after lunch, we're disappointed to find it doesn't hang right – my cheap fabric is too flimsy. Pam suggests sewing something into the hem to weigh it down and I find a heavy old chain in the barn. It makes a wonderfully spooky noise as it drags along the ground behind Fred – perfect for the ghostly statue.

By Wednesday, Fred has got Acts One and Two set. He leaves the cast to go through their arias and duets with Siobhan and Ben. Since he's only on stage in the first act and the last (the Commendatore is busy being dead in between) he's free to join Pam and me on our trip to Montluçon to fetch the costumes.

Fred is grudgingly impressed by the costumes we've selected. He points out that I've missed a nightdress for Donna in Act One. I haven't, I've got a long white nightie at home that we can use. Fred rejects the jackets we've chosen for Don Giovanni and Leporello pointing out that they'll be too hot in them. We select long Eighteenth Century waistcoats instead. We drive home with the boot and the back of the car stuffed to the top with lumpy bags of costumes and a froth of petticoats.

On Thursday morning Pam and I catch any member of the cast who is not actually singing to try things on. It's wonderful to see them take a deep breath and transform into their roles in front of the mirror. Philip, in particular, looks every inch the wicked seducer. Fred comes in fussing over the fact we have two identical black cloaks for the Don and Leporello. They will need to exchange cloaks when they impersonate each other, how is the audience going to tell which is which?

Later that day, I delved into my squirrel's hoard of braids and bindings. A tiny attic room too small to use as a bedroom has become our emporium of fabric, lacework, ribbons, braids, fringes and bindings. I emerged with a roll of scarlet satin edging. There was enough to go up, around and down the front of the Don's cloak. We gave Kate the job of hand stitching it on.

Just as we got Phil into his cloak we heard a 'Coo-coo' in the Hall. Roselyne had turned up with the hats. I was stunned. They were beautiful heavy black felt tricornes – perfect 18th Century hats. They had even been made to fit. Didier, Roselyne's husband insisted we measured the boy's heads to his precise instructions. With his hat on, Phil looked the business. Nic came by and did a real double-take.

Nic has been strangely absent from the kitchen this year. I assume that having the part of Don Ottavio is pretty heavy for him. He's probably learning his lines or practising his singing or something. But, the saucepans, Pam and I are missing him.

There are other undercurrents at work which I don't quite understand. I've overheard vague mutterings from the cast. It seems Ben feels everything is going too fast. He wants extra rehearsal time to go over the ensembles. Donna and Helen don't seem to be getting along. I ask Fred about it. 'It's a soprano thing,' he says in his ambiguous way. Soprano's seem to be a highly strung species. If there are rifts setting in, Jane and Fred are anxious to keep them from us. In fact, I'm starting to suspect that a lot is being kept from us.

All of a sudden it's Friday, just twenty four hours to go before the performance. Fred and Kate are coming to me with demands thick and fast.

'Is it all right if we take the big table from Peter's study?'

'You can, but it's terribly heavy. I can find you a lighter one.' No, for some reason, it has to be that table.

Can we have the pewter platter from the hall, and the bell, and some tankards and you wouldn't happen to have a cooked pheasant, would you?'

I seem to be doing six things at once. One of which is trying to set up a fan in the cellar, which Fred has designated as the location of Hell. The cellar has a little window on to the courtyard. I try to attach some red ribbons to a fan which should look reasonably like flames. Fred doesn't seem impressed by this. I feel a bit put out, that it has been left to me to worry about the special effects.

That afternoon, Peter, Pam and I hurry through our various duties.

We want to be free that evening to watch the entire run-through. This is going to be difficult. With the sudden escalation of tasks that always pile up at the end of the week, we've got our hands full. Peter has had to do a last minute reprint on his programmes and they all need collating and folding. The chairs and tables have arrived from the Mairie and someone has to set them out in the courtyard. I call M. Aubertin who turns up with his son and takes on this task. Pam is making last minute adjustments to the costumes. Donna has tried on my long white nightie in her room and come down scarlet-faced saying it won't fit.

'But that's ridiculous, it's really loose.'

'Not everywhere,' says Pam with a raised eyebrow. Pam takes the nightdress off to the sewing room and sorts it out, earning herself a new title: 'Queen of the Gusset.' There's nothing Pam can't let out - she's sewn a couple of inches of extra white material into the side seams and hey-presto its 12B bust measurement has grown to a healthy 14E. As I mentioned before, big boobs seem to be a defining feature of sopranos.

Pam and I get the spaghetti sauce ready and the spaghetti is measured out ready to be boiled. By 7 pm she, myself, Peter, Marjorie and Connie are chivvied to the front of the house where a row of seats have been set out for us.

'But I thought the First Act was meant to be in the courtyard,' whispers Peter as the opening notes of the overture ring out from the house.

'Shhhh!'

We watch as one by one the characters emerge from the house. Donna appears in an open window (in my nightie) and blows a kiss to Nic, dressed as Don Ottavio below. Jane, dressed as Zerlina in the peasant costume she bought at ENO, sidles across the front of the house with a big basket of vegetables.

'Hang on, those are my courgettes,' says Peter. We shush him again. Masetto follows her and they have a snog in the main doorway. The door is opened by a furious Commendatore (Fred) who sends them packing. The door is closed. Donna Anna pulls the curtains to, there is a pause and then Dan (Leporello) saunters on to the scene. He casts a glance up at Donna Anna's window and launches into the opening aria.

Our house has been transformed into the Commendatore's mansion. I'm seeing Gozinière in a whole new light. Suddenly it feels as if we're back in the 18th Century, I wouldn't be surprised if a horse and carriage drove up. There are more surprises in store, but Fred's being really secretive. We switch to the courtyard and watch the next act, but for some reason we're not allowed to see the final acts until tomorrow's performance.

The following morning, Saturday and the day of the performance, I come downstairs to find Fred asleep on the sofa in the sewing room.

'What on earth are you doing here?'

'Oh, strange night. Don't ask.'

I don't. But of course Pam gets the lowdown. It seems, the night before, Nic had an assignation with someone who shall be nameless. So that's why he was never around to do the saucepans! It's all becoming more than a little mysterious. Those undercurrents are running deep.

At around eleven Dan asks me if it would be all right to make a phone call on the landline to the UK.

Nothing wrong I hope?'

'No, nothing like that. I'm expecting a letter at home, that's all.'

I leave him to make his call in peace, something in his manner implies the call's important. Later, when we ring the bell for lunch, he's nowhere to be seen.

I find Jane in the kitchen loading a plate: 'What's happened to Dan?'

I'm taking a plate of food up to him. He's had a bit of bad news.

'Oh dear what?'

She frowns and leans a little closer, whispering; 'He's failed his finals at Guildhall.'

I stare at her in disbelief. Dan is brilliant. He's one of the best singers we've ever had. He has a gorgeous voice, he's very professional and he has real acting ability.

'I can't believe it.'

She shrugs. 'Nor can he.'

'Will he be all right for tonight?'

'Absolutely. But he doesn't want to face the others for a bit.'

'Can he do a retake?'

'I don't know. He may have to repeat a year.'

I realise the implications of this. Another year, another set of fees, another year without earning a living. It's a tough life for a singer.

The cast has been allowed Saturday off as usual to relax before the performance. It's a pretty hot day and most of them spend the afternoon beside the pool. Up at the house, it's all systems go as the tables are set up and laid on the lawn. Pam and I have learned a lesson from last year and I've put in a huge order of rare roast beef with the local butcher. He's cooking it and slicing it. I'm going to make a sauce of sour cream and horseradish brought over from the UK. The first course is duck paté which we've ordered from a local farmer's wife. And the dessert is coming from the village patisserie once again. We're pretty popular in the village this year. All we have to do is provide the salads.

We hear raucous sounds coming from the swimming pool. The cast seem to be having a whale of a time but I can see Fred moochg about alone down at the end of the lawn. Pam goes to have an O.P. with him.

'Is he OK?'

'He's fine,' she reports. 'He's learning his part.'

'Why does he always have to leave it till the last minute?'

'That's Fred for you.'

Claudia turns up about four pm with her new friends - an assortment of 'English' Parisians. They're all, apart from Claudia, staying at the local inn. These are an improvement on the French Parisians - they actually come into the kitchen and shake hands and offer to help. There's one in particular, a tall fellow with floppy dark hair who's a bit older than the others. Ding Dong. But, hang on, he's brought a French girlfriend with him. He immediately rolls up his sleeves and helps Peter shift furniture in the salon to make a clear path through for the audience.

'Who's he?' I ask Claudia.

'Oh Nick. He's an architect I think.'

'Uh-huh?'

'Mu-um, he's got a girlfriend.'

'Oh? How long have they been together?'

'I don't know. Why?'

'Nothing.'

Pam has been watching me. 'You're not going to come over all Emma Woodhouse again?'

'Wouldn't dream of it.' Pam knows I'm an incorrigible matchmaker. But our girls are getting on. I've bought those three antique cots, I've been hiding them in the barn.

'What do you think of his girlfriend?'

'Well, she doesn't seem that interested. My spies tell me she's been down at the pool chatting up Phil.'

'Dear, dear, dear.' I slip out to the tables on the lawn and do a little surreptitious switching of place names.

By six the guests are starting to arrive. The English Parisians have been back to their inn, changed and arrived back making a bee-line for the drinks. The French are more restrained, they hang around having the obligatory ten minutes of polite glass-free conversation. Claudia is nowhere to be seen. Pam arrives with Connie and Loki who is looking very pleased with herself, wearing a large red bow.

The glasses of champagne are being passed round – we can still afford champagne at this point. I'm hoping all this will be making a positive impression on this Nick person. English-architect-mature - Hmmm. But there's still no sign of Claudia. I hope she's making herself look extra gorgeous.

We have even more guests this year as we've been making new friends. Victor and Linda, who are Parisians but neighbours during the summer, arrive with their three offspring, Valerie, Rachel and handsome Harry. I've had the rundown on Harry from Linda, he's finding it hard to hold down a job and is currently scraping by promoting parties.

Out of the corner of my eye I can see Nick has introduced himself to Valerie and Rachel. I can hear from a distance he speaks impeccable French but I can't actually make out what he's saying.

Peter's talking to me.

'What?'
'What's that dog doing here?'
'Ask Pam.'

He catches Pam. 'You are going to get rid of her by the time the meal is served?'

'Why? She's very fond of rare beef.'

Peter is about to make his speech and Claudia still hasn't turned up. Valerie, Rachel and Nick seem to be getting worryingly pally. And then just as Peter takes his speech out of his pocket, Claudia arrives. She walks straight across the lawn, picks up a bowl of cocktail snacks and offers them to Harry.

Out of the corner of my eye, I can see Harry and Claudia with their heads together and when the speech draws to a close they find seats side by side. Nick is at the far end of the row back with his girlfriend.

'What's up,' asks Pam, noticing my expression.

'Nothing.'

The overture and opening act end to enthusiastic applause and then we pick up our chairs and make our way through the house to the courtyard. I notice Nick is being a real gentleman carting three or four chairs for the girls. Claudia trails behind Harry carrying hers.

The act continues with Donna giving a winningly touching performance as Donna Anna. Helen is suitably strident as Donna Elvira.

I tense as Dan comes on stage. With true professionalism he has left his problems off-stage. He brings the house down with Fred's translation of Leporello's aria listing Don Giovanni's conquests, which is rather ruder than usual – well, it is a private performance. He ends on:

'But the highest common factor, is a virgin whose intacta.
And his favourite endeavour, is a woman dressed in leather,
Rich or poor, wife or whore, behind the door, or on the floor,
He's so quick, it's like a brick and he's not picky with his wick
He'll seize a chance behind a curtain, any creature with a skirt
on...'

I glance over at Marjorie. She's nodding happily out of time with the music, her hearing aids don't seem to have picked up the text.

The action moves on to the peasant wedding. Jane as Zerlina and Tom as Masetto are well into their duet when a car is heard coming up the driveway. I'm slightly vexed at this late arrival but not half as livid as Loki, who does her best to drown the singers out with furious barking. She is carried off in disgrace by Pam.

This has left Connie sitting alone at the end of the row. A happy chance as far as she's concerned, because as Don Giovanni comes to the end of the final aria of the act, he invites the entire audience to have dinner. He needs a lady to accompany him. He leans down and gallantly grasps Connie by the elbow and leads her through the house, slightly flustered, but triumphant, to where the dinner is waiting on the tables outside.

Marjorie gets to her feet with dignity. She doesn't actually say anything. But I can tell by the set of her back as I follow her through that she feels she's been upstaged.

I peer over at Claudia's table. The seating has been rearranged once again. Claudia is next to Harry and Nick is at the far end with Rachel on one side and Valerie on the other. I give up.

The dinner is fine. The wine is nice. The weather is wonderful. I try to ignore what's going on at the 'Parisian' table. We sit enjoying the last warmth of the setting sun. By the time the dessert arrives, dusk is drawing in and Jacqueline and her sisters bring candles out to the tables.

As darkness falls, there's a curdling scream from the shrubbery. Jane emerges, her blouse torn and her hair in her eyes. She looks pretty convincingly seduced. Act Three continues around us. It's a brilliant piece of theatre on Fred's part and he has taken us totally by surprise.

The next scene is back in the courtyard. We up-seats again and trail through to find the flowerbed in the far corner has been turned into a graveyard. Fred is perched on top of the pillar that's been nicked from my garden statue. His head and the cloak have been painted with drips of white paint that look like pigeon droppings. He has my medieval helmet ice bucket tucked under his arm. As long as he doesn't move, he makes a passable statue. His deep voice rings out with the ghoulish relish of the dead Commendatore. A ripple runs through the audience as he raises his arm, his acceptance of Don Giovanni's invitation to dinner is suitably chilling.

There's a five minute break and we turn back to face the terrace where Peter's library table is set for a solo diner. The moment everyone loves doesn't disappoint. The statue's crunching footsteps can be heard echoing through from the hallway. There's even an eery drag of chains.

I notice that Kate has disappeared from her position as page turner. She's probably gone to turn on my clever fan and flames arrangement. But no, Don Giovanni is being pinned down on the table. The Commendatore has him in his iron grip and is about to drag him down to hell. The cellar door is thrown open. A stream of evil-looking demons emerge. For a moment I'm totally at a loss. Who are these people? Six evil demons have been conjured out of nowhere. And then I realise it's the entire cast dressed in black leotards and tights, their faces blacked around staring white eyeballs veined in red. I catch a glimpse of Fred, his eyes glinting with delight from inside the cloak at our amazed expressions. The demons lift Don Giovanni shoulder high and carry him down the cellar stairs with shrieks of demonic laughter.

Wisely Fred has cut the final quartet. Nothing could top that for a finale. As the applause breaks out, even Marjorie has her sang-froid back. Loki has been released and joins the cast on stage to take her bow - after all, she did have a vocal part.

Chapter Twelve

Breakfast the following day was the usual muted affair. As ever, the cast has drunk too much. There is no performance at the Terrays' this year. Their bookshop has closed due to competition from a large and vulgar LeClerc which has opened practically next door. I'd been to Moulins to check it out and found to my disgust that practically the whole ground floor was taken over by glossy books of cartoons – or 'bandes dessinés' as they call them – a French obsession that totally passes me by – they seem to think they've elevated it to an art form. I drove back home mourning for the loss of the Terray's lovely bookshop.

Peter's colleagues from advertising are starting to retire which means that more English people than ever have made the trip over to France to join us this year. Towards lunchtime they start to turn up at the house, full of enthusiasm and congratulations. By twelve-thirty the courtyard is quite crowded.

'We're going to have to feed them,' I whisper to Pam.

'What on? The supermarket closed at twelve.'

'Wasn't there some beef left?'

Loki is at our feet licking her lips.

'There's salad in the garden.'

'There's tons of bread left. And cheese – there's loads of cheese.'

'They've come all the way from England. We can't just give them bread and cheese.' I'm trying to make a rough estimate of how many mouths we have to feed.

'Ham,' says Pam with sudden inspiration.

'What do you mean ham? We haven't got any ham.'

'I'll be back in a minute,' she says and drives off in her car. She returns ten minutes later with ten tins of Ye Olde Oak Ham.

'Where did you get these? They're English.'

Pam is already tugging the pull-strip off one. 'Tell you later.'

'How old are they? They're not past their sell-by are they?' I search a tin suspiciously.

She's not listening, she's slicing a tinful on to a serving plate and arranging sprigs of parsley artfully around it. She sends me out to the vegetable plot to get salad and tomatoes. I'm not arguing, another carload of friends has turned up and the cast is lingering round the kitchen door like a pack of starving jackals.

I try a bit of ham on Loki. She wolfs it down and looks up for more. I wait for a minute to see if she's going to fall flat on her back with her legs in the air and when she doesn't, I try a bit. It tastes fine. It smells fine.

'It is fine!' says Pam and sweeps into the dining room with an armful of ham-laden plates.

Somehow we manage to feed around thirty people. Peter's ex-boss Ron has three helpings of ham and pronounces it the best ham he's had in years. I watch people anxiously during the afternoon but there don't seem to be any ill effects. They're all still fine by the evening. The English have disappeared. The Parisians have gone back to Paris. Peter is driving the cast down to Clermont Ferrand. Pam and I are in the kitchen washing up.

'You know they found tins of food from the Scott's Antarctic exploration ten years after Scott disappeared,' she said. 'When they opened them they were still perfectly fresh.'

Me, unimpressed: 'Really?'

'And they found a frozen mastodon in the permafrost in Siberia and the wolves were eating it,' she added.

'But you can still get salmonella from an undercooked burger,' I say. 'How 'Old-ee' was the ham anyway? I haven't seen that brand in years, it must be past its sell by.'

'No it's not.'

'It must be.'

Pam paused from the washing up.

'It can't be. It didn't have a sell-by. So it must be all right.'

'You can't mean it's pre-sell-by? Where did you get it?'

'Umm, Noel bought it.'

'Ten tins of Ye Olde Oak Ham?'

'No, he bought four hundred tins.'

'What! Why?'

'It was in the 'Seventies, or it may have been the 'Sixties. There was a scare. There was going to be a food shortage, can't quite remember why. Noel and a friend rang up the Ministry of Food and Fisheries and said that, if there was a famine, what would be the best thing to store?'

'And they said tinned ham?'

'Exactly.'

'Thank god I didn't know that when we served it.'

'You can be very ungrateful.'

The history of the ham has a sad end. Pam stored it in her barn. Every now and again a tin would be brought out. Peter and I banned it from the house but Pam ate it and it never seemed to do her any harm. The tins survived the minus 16C temperatures we had one winter. They survived the 'canicule' – the terrible heat wave we had in 2003. They survived the deluge the following spring when it rained solidly for three weeks. But the barn didn't do so well. One day Pam appeared for lunch looking shaken.

'I was in the house. I heard this terrible rumbling noise and came out to find the barn had collapsed.'

'Oh my god. No!'

'Well not quite all of it. Only one end.'

'Thank goodness you weren't inside.'

'Umm. I know.'

'What was inside?'

'Oh nothing much. A few old deckchairs. A sofa we threw out…And… Oh no!'

'Not the ham?'

'It must be buried under the rubble.'

'Thank god for that.'

Later that year the singers had a second performance of Don Giovanni in England. I now realised why Fred had been so against hiring the costumes, they had to hire them all over again. We'd given them all the props and The Commendatore's cloak and helmet. It caused a bit of a panic at the airport, setting off the alarms, the security guards confiscated the chain.

'Maybe,' I said to Pam. 'Maybe next time we should try and make the costumes.'

'We?' said Pam. 'So there is going to be a next time?'

'Fred's already talking about The Magic Flute.'

'You'll never have time to make them with all the cooking and everything.'

'But you could make them. I'll just take the credit.'

With more performances in England, our troupe was starting to feel more like a real opera company. They needed a name. Jane has emailed everyone asking for suggestions

Since they were always on the move I suggested: 'Foxtrot Opera.'

'Initials F.O?' said Peter.

'Maybe not.'

'Why don't you call them 'Gozinière Opera'?' suggested Marjorie.

'But the company have other performances besides coming here.'

'Pam's People's been taken,' said Pam.

We put our heads together and sent them a list: Impromptu Opera. Pocket Opera. Hat Trick Opera. Open Door Opera, Penny Opera, Twopenny Opera. Sit-up Opera.

Then a few days later an email from Jane came back with the final choice. Peter stomped downstairs from his study, his face a picture.

'You'll never guess what. They've called it after that bloody dog.'

'Called what?' said Marjorie.

'Opera Loki!'

Loki leapt to attention, her ears pricked: 'Did anyone mention my name?'

The Autumn rains set in. Pam and I took Loki for walks huddled in raincoats and gumboots. Loki loathed the rain, she tippy-toed round all the puddles, stopping every now and again for a good shake. Claudia has suggested we get her a raincoat. They have mini-Burberry ones on sale for dogs apparently, in Galeries Lafayette.

'Rubbish,' says Pam. I'm going to teach that animal how to behave like a dog.'

Loki looks up at her under her long eyelashes. She's going to have a job on her hands.

Marjorie is complaining about the cold again. Whatever we do to the house, the cold seems to find a way in. I check with the doctor and he says it will be fine to take her to Australia one more time. Her mobility has gone downhill and Juliet says she can't manage her in the house but she's found an alternative. Amazingly, a nearby old people's home is willing to give respite care to the relatives of local residents.

As soon as we get to Australia, Marjorie seems to perk up. One of the carers comes to interview her to make sure the home is appropriate for her. I'm starting to worry that they'll think she's too fit to be cared for. I sit in on the interview.

'Now, Marjorie, we're just going to ask you a few questions, dear. How's your hearing?'

'What?'

The interview continues through questions on legs and loos and teeth - false or otherwise and various dietary requirements. There's a little surprise over the fact that our local French doctor has prescribed her two glasses of red wine a day, preferably Burgundy. But the interview seems to be going pretty well. The kind carer ends with…

'And do you have specs?'

There's a pause from Marjorie.

'Oh no dear. Not any more. I'm far too old for that sort of thing.'

With Marjorie being cared for and all the tasks of Gozinière far away on the other side of the world, I find time to write. I've set up a table in the bedroom and tap away on my portable. I'm well into my book about the history of Gozinière. Shortly before we left for Australia I'd been introduced to a fellow whose house had belonged to a distant branch of the family who had lived for two centuries in our house. He'd confirmed, as I thought, that when they fled the Revolution, they'd gone to London. I'd managed to fit in a week of research at the British Library en route for Australia and had unearthed fascinating stories about the daily lives of French émigrés in London. Having fled with little more than the clothes on their backs, their jewellery and any small portable valuables they could lay hands on (snuff boxes were a favourite) the émigrés soon found they were short of money.

Aristocratic ladies who had never done more than petit-point, or playing the clavichord were forced to sew and embroider muslin dresses and make hats out of straw. The men had to look to their skills, teaching fencing or French; readings of French plays became really popular with London audiences. One ingenious fellow carved a miniature guillotine out of cherrywood and entertained the crowds with a ghoulish show where he beheaded ducks and geese, the unfortunate victims ending up as dinner each night.

By this time I'd pretty well decided to make a career change. I would stop writing books as I had for the past twenty years for teenagers and concentrate on adult fiction. Earlier that year I'd put forward a synopsis for a book about a High School in the year 3000 and Bloomsbury had flatly turned it down. Science Fiction was a niche market apparently and they were looking for their next best-seller. So I consoled myself by doing the opposite - delving back into the past. I'd been writing my book about our house in odd weeks stolen between the teenage books. As I met more of our French neighbours, more of its history was coming to light. It was becoming a bit of an obsession.

My research into the history of the house had one incredibly lucky side-effect. One of our newfound French friends introduced us to a fellow who was moving house and trying to downsize. I overheard him saying that he was having trouble getting rid of a baby grand piano. I pricked up my ears. We had a side room which we'd designated the music room since the singers liked to practice there. Normally they brought CD's of piano backing, but a real piano would be a tremendous bonus.

'We might be interested in buying your piano,' I said.

'Oh you wouldn't need to buy it,' he replied to my amazement. 'If it would help your young singers, I'd like to give it to you. All you'd need to pay for is the transport. That could be expensive.'

I exchanged glances with Peter. 'Well we would love it if you're absolutely sure. But we really should buy it.'

We did buy it in the end. The owner demanded a token one euro which would make the 'sale' official in the taxman's eyes. The piano was duly delivered a few weeks later. It had been in the music school of Versailles and the tuner who came to retune it after its journey gave it the seal of approval. Its soft pedal needed attention but apart from that it was in pretty good nick.

I put the euro into a little red velvet bag and invited the owner to our next opera where we would make the official handover.

But, back to the present. Marjorie and I returned from Australia rested, tanned and as I thought, in good health. At her advanced age Marjorie travelled Club Class. She treated me to a Club Class ticket as well. As I reclined in my Club Class seat in a lovely Vodka-and-Orange induced haze, a video of Madonna came up on my screen. I watched her with half an eye and turned the sound down. I suppose the Bloomsbury rejection must have been nagging at the back of my mind. An idea for a series of books just popped up like a surprise bubble over Madonna's head. What if a megastar like Madonna had a politically-correct daughter who was totally opposed to her mother? I gazed over at Marjorie – she had engaged the poor fellow in the seat next to her in conversation. 'Where was he going?' 'London! Oh so am I!'

It had huge comic potential. I even had a name for the book: 'My life starring Mum.' I quashed the idea. No, I was a real writer now – a writer of adult fiction. No doubt 'Lost&Found' (my book about Goziniere) would be snapped up by the first publisher I showed it to. It would probably be on Richard and Judy. I'd soon be composing my Booker Prize acceptance speech and making my selection of Desert Island Discs. AND I would no longer have to suffer those humiliating conversations that went something like this:

'I hear you're a writer?'

Me: 'Umm well, yes. Sort-of.'

'What do you write?'

Me: 'Books for teenagers mostly.'

'But how fascinating!...When are you going to write a proper book?'

Marjorie and I spent a couple of days in London recovering from the flight before returning to France. I took the opportunity to have lunch with Laura, my agent. It was the least I could do, she was going to suffer financially as well as I was, from the Bloomsbury let-down.

'I know you're disappointed, but you must have some other idea?' she said as we finished our coffee.

'No, not really. I mean I really want to finish this book about the house.'

'I can't represent it, you know. I only do children's books. It's a totally different market.'

This was a blow. I relied on Laura. She was always my first reader and critic. She was my greatest support. She had the task of selling all my work. And perhaps more importantly, she shielded me from criticism.

There was a pause. I was about to ask for the bill. A sudden vision of Madonna gyrating on the screen flitted through my mind.

'Unless…'

'Umm?'

'Well it's not much of an idea really but when I was on the plane…'

Laura's watching me intently as I outline the idea.

'…. maybe it could be called something like 'My life starring Mum?'

Laura put her coffee cup down on her saucer. 'I think it's a brilliant idea. Write me a synopsis. I'll put it up for auction.'

'Auction?'

'Yes, get all your publishers to put in competitive bids for it. That's how things are done these days. Why not?'

'But what about my book about the house?'

'You can write both, can't you?'

I wrote the synopsis, actually just doing that made me warm to the idea. Laura emailed to say she wanted synopses of three books. Publishers want series these days, everything's changed post H.P.

'I simply don't know why you want to write another book,' says Marjorie. 'Haven't you got enough to do as it is with the opera and everything. And you simply can't call it by that dreadful title.'

I stare at her realising that the idea for the book doesn't really come from Madonna at all. It's our relationship I'm writing about. We are so-oo different. I point out that I can hardly call the book 'My life starring Mummy.'

'I don't see why not.'

I'm still having second thoughts about writing another teenage series but the wheels have been set in motion. It's all happening very fast. Three publishers have put in sealed bids. Bloomsbury wins (serves them right). I come down to lunch the following day and announce that we can afford the opera this year. In fact we can afford it for several years to come.

The following week I have to sit down and actually start writing. I'm hardly through the first chapter when the horrible truth dawns on me. A synopsis is one thing – it's all potential and the book you self-complete in your mind is always brilliant. Writing the actual book is quite the reverse – it's a load of toil and self-doubt with only the occasional glorious interlude when your fingers waltz across the keyboard typing out words that can only have been dictated from heaven. The horrible truth is that I don't know my Emmy from my Grammy. I may be a bit of a nerd about opera but I know absolutely nothing about popular music. I phone a college friend Gloria, she's a TV producer and her husband was a drummer in a band in the 'Seventies. They are both hyper-cool and so are their children. She promises to give advice but I hardly dare admit the depth of my ignorance.

Peter catches me looking very hang-dog.

'Book not going well?'

I pour out my problems. He can't help – his interest in pop music ended with the Beatles – or, to be fair, maybe the Rolling Stones.

He has a good suggestion though. He has a meeting coming up in London. He says he'll go into Waterstones and buy me as many biographies of pop personalities he can find.

Meanwhile, I can't help noticing that Marjorie isn't quite herself. She hasn't told me I should get my hair cut or put some make-up on or wear nice court shoes in weeks. One lunch-time she passes out at the table. I call the doctor and Pam and I somehow get her into her wheelchair and back to her room. She comes round but she's still quite floppy when the doctor arrives. He takes her blood pressure and listens to her heart and lungs then takes a blood sample and tells me whatever happens she's not to move. She's to stay in her chair with her feet up.

We settle her under a blanket and leave her to sleep. I creep back at fifteen minute intervals to check she's still breathing. I start to feel remorse for all the times I've been short-tempered or impatient or generally daughter-like to her.

At five o'clock she's still sleeping, her breathing doesn't sound right. I call the doctor again but only get his answer-phone. I make my way back to her room dreading what I will find. Her chair is empty.

'Would you like a cup of tea?' Marjorie's voice comes from her little kitchen. She's standing there, right as rain, making tea.

'The doctor said you've got to stay in your chair with your feet up.'

'Rubbish. I'm fine? But I've run out of biscuits.'

I'm just getting used to the idea that my mother isn't about to die when the doctor's car skids to a halt on the gravel outside the house. He comes to the door at a run.

'She has to go to hospital for a blood transfusion immediately.' Apparently Marjorie's red blood count is dangerously low. An ambulance comes for her and I follow it into the Hospital in Moulins with her suitcase.

This is the start of a couple of months of misery. One thing leads to another. I seem to be sitting in endless corridors, translating diagnoses of blood specialists and heart specialists and gastro-enteric specialists. They each find something different wrong with Marjorie but the fact of the matter is her body simply isn't coping any more.

Every day I drive to the hospital and sit by her bedside. It's pretty rough on her that no-one there speaks English. She spends most of the time asleep and I get through the biographies of Madonna and Michael Jackson and Annie Lennox in record time. Somehow their unreal world of fame and wealth form the perfect escape from the hospital's grim, neon-lit corridors. While I'm trailing stars on four-inch heels striding down red carpets, white shoe'd feet pass me by, squeaking on the linoleum. Nothing is quite real while Marjorie hangs between life and death. I try to cut myself off, concentrating on this alien world of stardom. I try to place myself in a stadium of screaming fans, living life in the glare of camera flashes, fighting off publicity hungry journalists, surviving car chases and pouting for press pictures. But every few minutes I come back with a jolt to the miserable present.

When the hospital rings one evening to say Marjorie has died, I can't help feeling relief. In the last few days she'd made it clear she didn't want to go on living any longer. Her life ended with a series of strokes, the last of which was final.

I go into the hospital to pick up her things and a nurse comes in to ask me for her clothes - I'm a little taken back, Marjorie isn't going anywhere. In France apparently people are dressed up in their best clothes to be viewed in their coffin. I think this is a ghoulish idea and I say so.

I get lovely letters and emails from the singers. Marjorie had become a favourite with them over the years. They were always dropping in to her room for a chat and a drink and probably a little topping up as well. I dare say she heard more of their confidences than I ever did. But if so she kept them to herself. She always adored boys rather than girls. Some of the boys' stories must have come as a bit of a surprise.

In May Peter took me on a holiday to cheer me up. He had decided on America. I'd never been there. He had several friends and former colleagues he wanted to visit and crucially we would be able to catch up with Leo in L.A. I also wanted to do some on-the-spot research on the world of pop celebrities. Leo is living just off Sunset Boulevard and has promised to show me the city's most glamourous venues, where my heroine would no doubt hang out, and take me on some movie sets.

We arrive to find Leo in the throes of moving. She's taken a flat with Ben, an old friend from college. The two of them sharing means she can afford a much better apartment. The block they've chosen has its own swimming pool and a garden full of palm trees. She's busy unpacking boxes when we turn up at the new flat. We sit on packing cases and drink mugs of tea. Ben, seems a nice enough fellow but a mother's instinct tells me there's no romance likely here. Just as we're about to leave however, Charlie - a friend of Ben's - turns up.

He's tall and tanned and rather exotic. He also has a lovely smile and talks politely and listens to what Peter's saying with interest. I cast a meaningful glance at Leo, she's in baggy jogging pants and fluffy slippers, gorgeous as she is, this is not her best look. Leo doesn't seem to have noticed how yummy Charlie is. In fact, she seems to be doing her best to get rid of him. I'm about to take the initiative and offer him a cup of tea when I decide against it.

'He was nice,' I say to Leo, when he's gone.

'Was he?'

'Yes!'

Leo doesn't seem to be impressed.

I leave her flat with Peter and have a good old moan about the fact that we're never going to get our daughters married off.

'All in good time,' he says.

I think of my three antique cots gathering dust in the garage. Pity.

But we've more pressing problems. On Peter's daily email check he's found one from Jane. She's busy casting for 'The Magic Flute' but there's a problem with the pianist. Siobhan says she simply can't afford to come to France for a week, unpaid.

'It's an exhausting job,' says Peter.

He's right, the pianist is working all the time. Even when the cast is not on stage, the pianist will be going over arias and duets with individual singers.

'Maybe we should pay her then. How much does she want?'

'But that's not fair on the others. What about the Director or Jane? She works all-year-round as producer. What about the cast?'

The singers were growing up. They weren't students any more. They had commitments, rent, heating, fares… We tried to tot up what it would cost to give them all a basic fee. It came to a lot.

'Maybe we should stop right here. It's been wonderful. We've been terribly lucky. But if they need paying and start having babies and getting mortgages and things…'

After discussing it back and forth, Peter said he'd reply to Jane, saying that maybe we should cancel the opera this year. As much as we'd love to pay the pianist we really couldn't afford to pay everyone.

And we couldn't pay one member of the cast and not the others.

'I thought it was too good to last,' he ended.

We left L.A. feeling pretty miserable. The singers' visit had become really important to us, without the opera to look forward to, the year stretched ahead feeling blank and empty.

Peter had booked us a train journey across the U.S. to Chicago and then on to New York. The train chugs slowly, in fact very slowly through some of America's most stunning scenery. We see the lights of Las Vegas in the night. We cross a dust bowl desert and then climb slowly up a mountainside where it starts to snow.

The train actually isn't up to much. I'd envisaged a rail trip across the States as rather stylish, but our fellow diners were mainly ageing railway buffs and the food served reminded me of school dinners. Now and again one of the buffs would get into the engine room and treat us to a monologue over the sound system about the age, speed and relative velocity of USA's historic trains.

After leaving Chicago our train journey takes us through the backyard of America - a desolate world of rubbish dumps, derelict cars and trailer parks. One morning, memorably, we pass a ships' graveyard - endless rows of hulks are at anchor waiting to rust away into the sea. Rust to rust, ash to ashes, this is a coming-to-terms trip for me.

When we reach New York, Peter is back in email contact. There's an email from Jane. She says she quite understands. She and the singers who come to Gozinière are perfectly happy to treat the week as an opera course. In fact, singers often pay to go on such courses in order to develop their repertoire. Touchingly, she adds that the week with us is the best week in her year, she looks forward to it all year round. She's sure she'll find another pianist, so please, please don't cancel this year.

'I just hope M.Aubertin's dug the plot over,' says Peter. 'I'll have to get planting when we get home.'

Back in France I have to pull myself together and look to the future. I redecorate Marjorie's room and buy a new double bed for it. This summer we'll have an extra bedroom for the singers and Marjorie's sitting room will provide a Green Room where they can make their teas and coffees and keep from under our feet while we're cooking.

I email Jane to tell her the good news that she won't have to share a bed this year, she can have Marjorie's room. She emails back to say: 'Anywhere else, please. It would be just too sad to be in her room.' She adds the brilliant news that Roland has agreed to spend a week of his precious holiday as musical director and pianist for us – on the condition that he can bring his new 'partner'.

We email back to say we're thrilled he's coming and of course he can bring his friend. This means one more mouth to feed; I just hope his friend will lend a hand with the production. So Marjorie's room goes to Roland. It's a good thing it's on the ground floor!

I'm starting to worry about the props. How on earth is Fred going to do the trials by fire and water? I email him. Fred replies airily, not to worry, he's got it all worked out, could he have some money towards the costumes? He's bought bales of cheesecloth incredibly cheaply in Brick Lane market which he has been busy dying and is making what he calls 'timeless robes'. Pam mutters something about hoping they're 'timeless' enough not to fall apart on the night.

News of Opera Loki is circulating through the world of singers and there is plenty of competition for the leading roles. I think the key words 'swimming pool' and 'ample food and wine' may be helping with the casting. Jane says we are in for a treat with the new tenor they've found: Tyler Clarke. Philip Spendley has agreed to come back this year and so has Nic. It has been tricky casting The Queen of the Night - Kitty is a mezzo, so out of the question. Donna is playing the Queen of the Night's daughter - Pamina. And Jane is taking the comic part Papagena. A week or so later we hear that she's found a girl called Jess Killick who is a coloratura soprano and can reach those top 'C's with ease. Fred has cast himself in the key role of Sarastro – I suspect this may have something to do with his enthusiasm for the opera. Jane, Kitty and a new girl Alison are to play the Queen of the Night's three henchwomen and also the three boy trebles.

The opera will be a little earlier than usual this year, on the 31st July. We are hoping to thwart the summer storms by getting in before they start. Fred is planning to set the whole opera outside, so the weather is crucial. As the day of their arrival approaches we scan the weather forecasts. It seems we're in luck – fine weather is predicted for the entire week of the rehearsals and the night itself.

We brought a little stone statue of a flautist with us when we moved from London. It is practically buried in foliage in the garden and nicely aged. (I kept M. Aubertin and his scrubbing brush well away from it). This forms the image on the invitation and programme.

Acceptances are already coming in. This year the audience will be bigger than ever.

I ring Claudia to tell her she'll have to restrict the number of friends she brings this year.

'I can bring one though, can't I?' ('Beastly Julien', is still lingering in the wings.)

'Who?'

'Erm, do you remember Nick?'

I try to keep my voice level: 'What's happened to the girlfriend?'

'History.'

'Oh? So… are you two..?'

'No.. nothing like that. He just happened to say he enjoyed coming to the house.'

'When?'

'Last year.'

'No, when did he say that?'

'When we had lunch together.'

'Lunch?' (Not dinner - pity) 'And?'

'And nothing! He said he'd come round and put a shelf up for me.'

I go and tell Peter the good news.

'So, he's putting a shelf up. Do we need to call the bans?'

'But a shelf. He's making an effort. He wouldn't do that if he wasn't interested, would he? I mean a shelf is something permanent…' I tail off.

'As long as she's not on it,' mutters Peter.

It takes a minute or so for me to get this.

So Claudia's bringing Nick. Does that mean two beds or one? I go and take another look at my bedroom plan. Leo's still in L.A. so I don't need a room for her. She's being a bit mysterious too. Every time I ring the apartment, Ben answers and he gets Leo to call me back.

As soon as the cast arrive, they settle into the house as if it's their home. Nic and Kate take charge of Marjorie's kitchen and a car is dispatched to the supermarket to stock up on 'essentials'. The following day when I go over to replenish the milk, I find their fridge packed to the gills with snacks, biscuits, pains au chocolat and a large pot of Nutella. This is odd because Fred claims to be on a diet. It's a slightly inconvenient diet as it means he eats different things on alternate days. Farinaceous, fruit and veg on one day and meat, fats and other proteins on the other. Pam and I are already feeling a little frayed over our menus because we also have a couple of non-pork eaters – could be religious - and a vegetarian (they don't understand vegetarians in France). To cap it all, Alison is suffering from some rare allergy that means she can't eat anything dairy or wheat-based. It's going to be quite a challenging week catering-wise.

Somehow, we manage to cobble a dinner together that will suit everyone. We have two curries, one vegetable and one chicken, a bowl of dahl and plenty of rice. Diet or no diets, it all disappears. We linger with the cast after dinner enjoying the last of the sunlight - the evenings are long in July.

As I said earlier, the cast is growing up. The conversation turns to jobs and careers. They quiz Peter and me on our lives in advertising.

I tell them I was lucky enough to be really unsuccessful at work (I managed to be fired twice from the same agency) so I was forced to do something else – write books. Pam has never worked in an office, she's had a series of different careers including owning a leather shop, running a restaurant and apprenticing herself to an upholsterer to learn the trade. Peter points out that all these skills have been invaluable to Opera Loki.

The cast come up with a colourful range of day jobs: Phil Spendley turns out to be a zoo keeper. Nic works at a call centre for a bank – I just hope I get someone as sweet as him on the end of the line the next time I go into the red. He's planning, however, to train for an acting career and has applied for a scholarship in musical theatre at the Guildford School of Acting. Kate is now a chartered physiotherapist with a key post in a leading London Hospital. Jane has moved on from her ad agency job in Dublin to become a freelance marketing manager. Roland has his successful career in a top accountancy firm. Fred is still teaching but hoping to save up enough money to join Nic at Guildford. Kitty doesn't have a day job, she's going to move in with her partner who is also an opera singer and somehow they hope to get by on professional singing engagements. The most surprising of all is Donna. She's working in the Control Room of the London Underground. It'll be crime if her vocal performances are restricted to 'Mind the Gap' and 'Please stand clear of the approaching train.'

I move to a seat beside her: 'But surely you should be going to music college?'

'I'm not sure if I can get in,'

'But of course you can.' We all insist.

Donna's still hesitant. 'Besides, I don't think I can afford it.'

Peter and I are becoming all too aware of the precarious nature of the singers' lives. They are all incredibly talented, and impressively committed. Most of them play an instrument at a professional level as well as singing. Apart from Fred and Donna, they've all been to music college, gaining places in the face of tremendous competition. They've spent three years self-financing themselves for their first degree. And most have spent a couple more for a Masters. At the end of this they're lucky to get a chorus part in a minor opera company. These parts are poorly paid and they often have to travel miles and attend rehearsals before they earn a penny. In the meantime, even if they have no professional engagements, they still need to pay for classes with their singing teachers.

We didn't start out with the objective of helping singers. It was all done pretty thoughtlessly, putting on the operas just for the love of music and the fun of it. But we are now starting to realise that we need a more considered objective. We'd love to help each and every one of them. But there's no way we can afford to fund people like Donna through college. We talk to Jane about making Opera Loki into a charity. She says she'll look into it and we promise to talk it through with our accountant on our next visit to London.

Meanwhile we've got an opera to put on. The following morning Kate arrives at the kitchen door with an armful of shimmering sari silk.

'Fred wants us to make a dragon.'

I hand my tea towel to Pam and follow her over to the barn which we've designated prop. headquarters. Fred's idea is to make the dragon by sewing the long length of sari fabric to a series of hoops. The cast will hold them aloft and form the legs, winding the body of the dragon back and forth as they do in Chinatown parades.

The main problem is the head. We discuss the various options: paper-maché plastered over a balloon? Chicken-wire and Polyfilla? In the end we make a cardboard sculpture of the head with a mouth that opens and closes showing a double set of cardboard teeth. I leave Kate to paint the whole thing and make a long silly lolling tongue. We're rather proud of the final effect and call Fred to admire it.

'It's meant to be scary not comic,' he points out. So it's back to the drawing board. We add some evil ping-pong ball eyes – now where did we get that idea? And add a coat of shiny scales to make it look more reptilian.

Our next job is Papageno's bird catching equipment. I've bought what looks like a birdcage made out of hazel twigs – it's actually a conical plant support but it makes a wacky kind of birdcage when attached to a stick by a chain. Juliet has arrived from Australia. She'd planned the trip to see Marjorie, now sadly it's a trip to see us instead. Still jet-lagged she asks for a job – we give her the not too taxing task of making the birds to go in the cage.

I'm still worrying about the trials by fire and water. Fred says for the fire he wants a load of flares to go down each side of the courtyard and Peter is sent to Moulins to buy them. He comes back with some nicely timeless-looking bamboo ones and we set M.Aubertin to making holes for them in the gravel. Peter has bought a big canister of lamp oil but just as we are about to fill and test the flares, we find this has mysteriously disappeared.

I track it down to a little secluded area behind the barn. I find Fred and Roland busy making an odd kind of wand out of bamboo with a piece of rag wound round the end.

'What's that for?' I ask.

'It's a surprise,' says Fred, casting a furtive glance at the canister of oil.

I put two and two together.

'Not fire eating?'

'It's perfectly safe. You don't actually swallow the oil,' says Fred.

'Cracheur du feu – that's what the French call it,' says Roland, knowledgeably. 'It's a trick. You spit the oil at the flame.'

'It can't possibly be safe.'

Fred has a box of matches in his hand. Roland bends down and soaks the rag end of the wand in the oil. I try to intervene: 'I'm sure you need training for this or a licence or something.'

I'm being ignored.

'Stand back.'

I do just in time as Roland blows a very impressive-looking flame.

I have hideous visions of Roland swallowing rather than blowing and literally exploding. Not to mention the fact that with an audience, it must be a Health and Safety hazard. We should probably have the local fire brigade standing by. I go and find Peter to back me up. I'm sure someone is going to loose their hair or vocal chords or some other vital body part.

With pressure from both of us, Fred and Roland back down. I confiscate the oil and take it back to M. Aubertin. It's dark by now and once the flares are lit, they make a very impressive scene with the dancing flames reflecting off the walls of the house.

'Look at that,' I say to Fred. 'There's no need for a fire-eater.'

The week progresses. We've fallen in step with Fred's rhythm. He likes a slow start to the day – plenty of thinking time with cigarettes and coffee. The morning is spent mainly in a side room we call the music room with individuals going over their arias with Roland at the piano. By lunchtime most of the cast have found their way to the swimming pool. We have to ring the bell hard to get them to the table. The serious rehearsing doesn't start until around three in the afternoon. By that time I've started cooking the evening meal. I throw the kitchen windows open and chop vegetables to the accompaniment of their voices. Kate once suggested that she and Jane should cook a meal to relieve me. I looked at them in horror. I love cooking, and cooking for a large group of hungry and appreciative eaters to the accompaniment of divine music, comes close to my idea of heaven.

After dinner, the really serious rehearsing begins. This is when Fred likes to do a run-through of each act. Peter, and I are on our knees by this time. We go to bed with our windows open and listen in the dark to the voices from the garden. More heaven.

The week seems to flash by. Suddenly we've reached the dress rehearsal and Fred's costumes come out. Actually, Pam and I have to admit he's done a good job. He's dyed the robes in a range of hot pinks, cinnamon, saffron and terracotta. Topped with turbans they're both earthy and timeless. The Queen of the Night has a long midnight blue cloak which he's spattered with a starry sky of fake gems. Pam and I add the finishing touches to Papageno's costume sewing on a fringe of cock pheasant feathers which I've saved from last autumn's game dinners. The three 'boys' i.e. Jane, Kitty and Alison, appear dressed in striped pyjamas, each holding teddy bears. Interesting…

The weather is being kind to us. Saturday dawns with a forget-me-not sky and not a cloud in sight. This is our fourth opera and we've ironed out a few wrinkles. Everyone has been appointed a specific task. I'm in charge of food – Pam's B&B is up and running and she's fully occupied with her house full of guests. They're our guests as it happens - she's putting up opera experts Ken and Charles and an assortment of other people. Reports from her house - L'Ombre - make me quite jealous, apparently meals are delicious and conversations outrageous. Two of her house guests, Carl and Veronica, have become regulars at our opera – they've taken on the job of table-laying. From the kitchen I can hear their voices as they squabble over which tablecloth fits where, and sort through my piles of brocante plates, rejecting the chipped ones. M. Aubertin and his son deal with the tables and chairs. Peter's responsibility is programmes and table plans, this year we've added cast biographies since the cast now have other performances to add to their C.V.'s – and of course there's his speech. Juliet is still trying to fix wings on Papageno's birds. She has a couple of ping pong balls and a bag full of feathers and her fingers are covered with glue.

At around lunchtime Claudia shows up, alone.

'Where's Nick?' I ask.

'Mu-um, we're not an item.'

This is bad news. Even worse there's a plaintive mewing sound from her car.

'Claudia!'

'That's Tyson.'

'Tell me it's not a cat!'

'It's not a cat – it's a kitten.'

Grrrhhhhhh!

So I have to find a kitten-friendly space in the house to lock him away from Peter. I can't deal with male rage at a time like this.

Somehow, by six o'clock, the food is ready, the tables are laid, candles are in all the candlesticks and Jacqueline and her sisters have arrived. I rush upstairs to have a quick bath. A cold one as it happens, as I'm the last to dress. I lie in the bath listening to the sounds of the house…

Roland is in the music room going over a tricky bit of the overture on the baby grand. I can hear Jess warming up, her arpeggios getting higher and higher and impossibly higher. There's Peter rehearsing his speech in faltering French. I can hear the deep throaty voice of Veronica who is double-checking the tables with Carl. And Kate calling down to Nic to plug a light into a socket. I can hear a faint plaintive mewing from the box room. And I can hear the first car arriving!

I leap out of the bath and do a lightening change. I've managed to get dressing and make-up down to less than ten minutes. I look like shit but people have come to see the opera, not me.

There are a few surprises and a bit of magic on the night. Fred's set the opening scene in a suitably sylvan location by the pond. When our dragon appears out of the shrubbery, with its tongue lolling, it gets a round of applause. It does look rather silly but then it's a pretty daft opera.

The magic bit comes when Papageno plays his flute to attract the birds. A ripple of laughter runs through the audience. On cue, our two ducks - Chekhov and Ibsen – have swum straight across the pond to arrive at his feet.

Jess makes an impressive entrance as the Queen of the Night. Fred's using that rough avenue of trees that M.Aubertin cleared leading up to the pond. She walks the length of it, her cloak flying out behind her, as she sings those cut-crystal notes.

Every time Tyler sings I get goose pimples. He's by far the best tenor we've ever had. Tenors are always a problem – while sopranos are two a penny (tough for them), good tenors are thin on the ground.

Jane's been incredibly lucky to cast Tyler, he's going on to great things, which means he'll probably never sing for us again. But this is the whole point of Opera Loki. We want our singers to move on. Our job is to provide a step up the ladder of a professional career.

'It's going well,' I whisper to Peter.

'So far, so good.'

We're refining our cast. And we're refining our audience too. We simply can't invite everyone. We're getting to know who actually enjoys the music and who simply comes for the social event. And who, like handsome Harry the year before (who spent the whole of Don Giovanni texting on his mobile), won't be invited again.

By the final act, I've totally relaxed – could be something to do with the wine at dinner. Since the weather is kind the dinner was set out on the lawn in front of the house. By the time we finish eating, which seems to get later each year, the shadows have gathered around us, candles flicker on the tables and we're surrounded by inky darkness.

The bell in the tower starts tolling. Kate, dressed in one of Fred's robes, comes out of the house holding a branched candlestick up high. There's a sudden hush from the guests around the tables. The audience is unusually quiet as she leads them through the house and out into the courtyard.

The flares are all lit, their flickering light is dancing over the ancient walls of the house. Above us, a ceiling of night sky is set with millions of stars – we're in Sarastro's Temple.

I notice people are talking in whispers as they settle in their seats. There's an almost religious tension as the music starts to play. We watch 'the trials of silence'. Papageno is united with Papagena, played by Jane with comic panache. At last, we come to the ordeals of fire and water. I can see M.Aubertin waiting in the shadows with a fishing line attached to the roll of blue silk that he's going to going to swish across the courtyard to form water. Roland is safely seated at the piano, so there's no way he can do any fire eating. I'm worrying about the water bit – M.Aubertin's slightly hard of hearing, he's never going to hear his cue.

The magic flute refrain has begun. Hang on, that's not the piano playing... Kate is standing by the piano playing her flute – playing it really well too. Where's Roland?

He's done a lightning change into robes and has appeared in the line of Sarastro's priests with that wand in his hand. I tense.
With that characteristic 'FWOOM' noise, he blows a stream of flames into the darkness. He doesn't choke. He doesn't self-combust. He can't set his hair on fire because he's wearing a turban. His circus act gets a round of loud clapping. I catch Fred's eye in the torchlight and frown. He's laughing at me. I give him a very disapproving 'health and safety' frown in return.

Sunday dawns on the usual trashed house. We've learnt from the previous year. There's no way I'm going to give umpteen people lunch. Pam's ham had been outlawed and I'm not going to start cooking again. A few weeks back Peter booked all the tables of a little local restaurant. We're going to treat the cast to lunch. Anyone else who turns up is welcome to join us.

'We ought to do something to thank them,' said Peter.

'You're not going to give a speech. You got so pissed last year you called some of the boys 'queer'.'

'Well they are, most of them.'

'They're not, they're gay.'

'You make a speech then.'

'OK I will. We'll have an Awards Ceremony.'

I'd started saving silly little presents I'd bought in brocantes. I had a couple of 18th C style figurines for Tamino and Pamina, two carved wooden ducks for Papageno, a cut crystal for The Queen of the Night and a load of little mementos for the others.

We rolled up at the restaurant with the cast in various stages of hangover. Donna had learned her lesson this year and had gone easy. Carl and Veronica and the rest of Pam's household joined us. I don't think our restaurateur had ever served a noisier clientele or had so much of his Côte du Rhone drunk at one sitting.

My 'Awards Ceremony' was greeted by whoops and cheers and some very drunken acceptance speeches. And then Jane got to her feet. She wanted to thank us. Each year they'd thought that the opera would be our last and each year we'd asked them back again. She said that when we thought of cancelling this year, her world fell apart. We were all getting a bit emotional by this time.

Peter was on his feet. I was groping for a tissue when I heard him say that 'we' wanted them back again next year. He and Fred had already been discussing the choice of opera.

This was news to me. I hadn't forgiven Fred for the fire-eating yet.

Chapter Thirteen

I spent the following Autumn trying to catch up on a backlog of writing. 'My Life starring Mum,' had come out and I was half way through the second book. This was set in L.A. Leo, acting as researcher, was reporting back on Hollywood parties that had me sighing over the list of canapés. These A-list events had thoughtful little extras like having a masked rider to accompany you to your table or LED lights in your champagne fountain or little designer going-home gifts from people like Gucci. It was all a far cry from our homespun operas. While basking in the vicarious glamour, I was also rather shocked in my Puritan way, by the extravagance of it all.

Unsurprisingly Leo was loving L.A. but it wasn't just the partying. I'd discovered why she was being so elusive on the phone. She wasn't spending much time in her apartment with Ben. She'd been over at Charlie's place.

I'd reached the nitty-gritty part of book two. The hard part when you're approaching the end, wondering if you've tied up all the ends in a satisfactory manner, or whether you're being horribly obvious and the conclusion is too contrived. In short, I was going through an average period of self-doubt, when the phone on my desk rang. It was Leo.

'Hi darling, how's things? Did you get me those shots of the W. Hotel's glass stairway?'

We chatted on about a lunch she'd had at Chateau Marmont (as one does) and then she said. 'Umm, incidentally Charlie... er proposed last night.'

The room spun. Calm. Self-control. Let her do the talking.

'What did you say?'

'Yes!'

I sailed down the stairs and went and found Peter digging on the allotment.

'Guess what.'

'What?'

'Leo and Charlie have got engaged.'

Peter straightened up and threw a potato into his canvas bucket.

'What did you say?'

'Leo and Charlie. They want to get married.'

'But she hardly knows him.'

I look at him pityingly. 'She's been there for over a year.'

'Has she?'

'Yes. And she's been sleeping at his place. She's never there when I phone.'

'Really? How do you know?' (Why are men so-oo slow about this sort of thing.)

'Well, where else could she have been?'

'Why doesn't anyone ever tell me anything?'

I feel like pointing out that I can't talk to him when he's in his study because he tends to press the wrong key on his computer and erase everything. I can't talk to him in the car because he's likely to drive into something. I can't talk to him when he's eating because he'll choke or bite his tongue. I can't talk to him in bed because he's generally reading the Spectator. And I can't speak to him when he's in the bath because he doesn't have his hearing aids in!

'But aren't you pleased?'

'Yes. Yes, I suppose I am. He seemed a nice enough chap.'

'I thought he was lovely.'

'You only saw him for five minutes.'

'That was enough.'

I go to the barn and have a quick gloat at my three antique cots.

Things are progressing nicely in Paris too. That shelf never did get put up. I had Claudia on the phone. Nick came round apparently and they decided to go out to dinner instead.

'Oh that's nice. Where did he take you?'

'We had a glass or two of wine and we never actually got to the restaurant.'

'Oh?'

I decide not to share this with Peter. He's had more romance than he can handle for a while. I'd better let the relationship mature a little first. I tell Pam though.

'Hmm,' she says. 'He's a bit of a Hugh Grant type.'

'He'd have to be to manage Claudia.'

'Hope he likes cats.'

Over the next few months, we discover Nick does like cats and it seems he likes Claudia too. She's making noises about her flat being far too small for her. Nick's renting his and needs to move on and they've started looking at property together. I hardly dare tell Peter. He's barely recovered from the last time she moved. A certain amount of baling out and topping up had to be done.

On the opera front, things have gone very quiet from Fred. He's applied to Guildford School of Music and Drama and been accepted. He's working round the clock to try and save up the fees.

Charlie and Leo fly to London and we drive over and meet them there and go out for a celebration meal. They tell us to our delight that they want to move back to the UK. They want to get married in Europe where all their friends live.

We're heading into winter and still no decision has been made about next year's opera. At last we've had an email from Fred. He's really proud of himself, he's lost 3 stone on his diet. I congratulate myself on my dietary education policy, Fred is my first big success. On a trip to Paris I buy him an 18th Century shirt in a shop in St Germain des Près as a reward. Being Fred of course, with his constant changes of lodgings, the parcel goes astray. Which is probably just as well as it wouldn't have fitted him for long. Three months later we hear that he's put the three stone back on again. But, as Pam points out, this is a different three stone.

One evening we have friends to dinner. I'm just carrying the first course to the table when the phone rings. Shall I leave it to go on to message? I don't, I put down the tray and answer it. I stagger back to the table and announce to Peter and our friends.

'That was Claudia. She's pregnant.'

Everyone is on their feet congratulating us. They all think this is splendid news. I take a sideways glance at Peter. He's accepting the congratulations as if he had something to do with it.

I can't help thinking how different things would have been when we were young. This news would have been greeted with shame and rage. Everything has changed in one generation. It's perhaps just as well Marjorie didn't live to hear this.

Peter is starting to make noises about Nick and Claudia. 'If they're buying a place together and having a baby, shouldn't they be getting married?'

He's voiced my thoughts but I say non-committally: 'Lots of people don't these days. Look at Gloria and Jake.' My best pal from college – Gloria has been happily unmarried to her partner Jake for thirty years, they've got four children.

Peter's not convinced by this.

'Well, if you want them to get married, you'd better talk to Nick man-to-man. That's your job.'

'He's forty-three. I can't tell him what to do.'

'Better get a shotgun then.'

Claudia and Nick are coming down the following weekend. I impress on Peter that this will be the ideal time to bring the subject up. He'd better start deciding what to say. In fact, it becomes even easier. Claudia's new cat, Tyson, is terrified of going in cars. Each time he's been taken to the vet, it's been a disaster at both ends (of the cat not the journey). The plan is for Claudia to drive down in the car and Nick to come by train with the cat in a basket. Tyson doesn't mind trains, Claudia assures us, they don't sway around like cars. And Nick has booked himself a First Class ticket, so the two of them can travel in style.

'So that's ideal,' I tell Peter. 'You can go and pick Nick up from the station and have a jolly good man-to-man talk on the way home.'

He's still looking doubtful.

'Do you want an illegitimate grandchild?'

'Well no but…'

'Good. Do it then.'

Peter leaves for the station. I get busy making a nice male-friendly feast. Claudia is driving down after work, she won't be with us till around ten. We'll have time to have a good chat with Nick. Ding dong, I fantasise to myself.

An hour or so later I hear the car arrive. I look out through the kitchen window. Peter gets out and so does Nick carrying the cat basket. They trudge across the gravel looking downcast. Nick puts the cat basket down outside. This isn't looking good.

I meet Peter's eyes and he shakes his head in negative. He goes to the cupboard and pours Nick a large whisky. Nick's disappeared to wash his hands. There's a muted miaow from outside.

'So what happened? Did you ask him?' I hiss at Peter.

'No, I couldn't.'

(Men!) 'Why on earth not?'

Nick joins us. Claudia was wrong about the cat and the train apparently. Tyson started puking and shitting a kilometre or so outside the Gare de Lyon. He continued, interspersed with yowling and scrabbling, all the way to Moulins. Nick got through a roll of kitchen towel cleaning up and apologies to his fellow first class passengers didn't go down too well.

'See. I couldn't possibly mention marriage, could I?' said Peter as Nick disappeared upstairs for a shower.

'I suppose not.'

I comfort myself by getting one of my antique cots out of the barn and lining it with fine blue checked material. Blue? Why not? We have two daughters; nature should do something to redress the balance.

Spring has come and Claudia and Nick have moved into their new flat. She got over the first three months of puking and was nicely swelling when Tyson redeemed himself. She was lying in bed one morning when Tyson came in with a small parcel attached to his collar. Inside was a ring, a nice ring – well Nick was a designer after all.

So we've not one but two weddings to plan.

Both the girls want to get married at Gozinière. As Claudia says: 'What's the point in having a big house if you don't use it?'

Nobody's asked me if I can manage two weddings. But as Pam points out: 'If we can knit an opera, we can surely knit a wedding.'

'Or two?'

That night I toss and turn trying to think of what to say to Jane. She and Fred will be so disappointed not to have an opera this year.

Then I turn over trying to work out how we can manage two weddings in one summer or whether we could persuade the girls to have a joint wedding or maybe two weddings back to back, meaning economies of scale.

The next morning when I email these alternatives to Claudia and Leo, I find the pressure is off. Claudia says she wants a proper white church wedding and doesn't want it until she gets her figure back, so the following year. Our future grandchild can be either a bridesmaid or page depending on sex. Leo wants a civil wedding in the Mairie but not until she and Charlie have moved back to the UK.

I track down Peter bedding in courgette plants.

'Thank god for that,' he says.

'Which means of course...'

'What?'

'We can have the opera after all this summer.'

Chapter Fourteen

It's already May and we still haven't decided on the choice of opera. Everyone has a different idea. Peter and I make a trip to London. We're taking Jane to a performance of 'Cosi fan Tutte' to try and convince her that this will be the best choice. We'll meet up with Fred for dinner after the performance to have a brainstorm.

Jane's impressed by Cosi but says the plot is weak and with the whole swapping over of lovers thing it's all too easy to get the characters mixed up.

Fred looks smug at this. He wants 'A little night music". He's been trying to convert us to music theatre from the very beginning. He insists that Sondheim is 'practically opera'. He sent us a CD to persuade us. We both loathed it. In particular the number, 'Bring in the clowns'.

'I think it's about the most maudlin and self-indulgent song ever written.' I hear myself saying. (Hang on, wasn't I meant to be being impartial?)

'So I guess that's a no-no then?' says Fred.

We play around with the idea of "Cabaret". Fred paints an exciting picture of the large attic done up as a night club and the audience sitting at little individual round tables.

'But we'll roast in the attic in August,' Peter points out.

There's a pause and I mention that I'd been getting a certain amount of flak about performing our operas in English.

'How about "The Rake's Progress"? I suggest. 'That's meant to be performed in English.'

'Stravinsky,' says Fred doubtfully. 'Not to everyone's taste.'

'Nor is Sondheim,' I point out.

'But it's perfect for the house.'

'Or Eugine Onegin?' suggests Peter. 'That's also set in a country house.'

'Tchaikovsky. We'd need an orchestra,' said Fred.

In the end we come back to Mozart. The divine strains of Cosi are still running through my brain.

'It really does have a daft plot,' says Peter.

'But a small-ish cast' I point out, thinking of all the meals. 'Catering-wise it's the ideal choice.'

'There's a part for each of us,' says Jane to Fred. 'You, me, Kitty and Donna.'

'Surely you can find some way to make the action easier to follow,' I add.

Fred looks doubtful. But we agree on Cosi unless he can come up with a better suggestion. Time is getting short.

A week or so later, we hear from Jane that Fred's all enthusiastic about Cosi. He wants to do an updated version, setting the opera in the 'Fifties and has 'ideas' about clarifying the characterisation and is suggesting 'interesting' locations for the various acts.

He's settled on the casting. Kitty and Donna are to sing the two sisters: Dorabella and Fiordiligi. Fred himself will play the conniving old fellow – Don Alfonso - who orchestrates the tangled love affairs. He's cast Jane as the worldly-wise maid Despina - his partner in crime. All they need to find now are two blokes for the two male lovers.

After a few false starts, we get the news that a tenor – Johnny and a baritone who has the rather extraordinary name of Yalmar, have been cast. Plus there's a final role which has been given to Nic. He's to be: 'Pool Boy.'

'There's never been a 'Pool Boy' in Cosi before,' objects Peter.

Pam and I want lovely Nic to come – this year his love life may even permit him to be an asset in the kitchen.

'It's probably something to do with billiards,' says Pam, so we leave it at that.

Fred has said he'll deal with the costumes. He has his own ideas and can source most things in the UK. But can we supply two military uniforms?

I have occasionally seen uniforms for sale at Emmaus. Fred's request means that Pam and I have a good excuse for our weekly sorties. As luck would have it, the very next Saturday I find a deep green military jacket in their Moulins saleroom and snap it up. When I get it home Peter examines it doubtfully. It's not a uniform he recognises from any army. It has a little gold instrument that looks like a trombone embroidered on one lapel. I decide to go and ask our neighbour François Civreis about it. We don't want half the audience walking out because we've dressed up one of our singers as a Nazi.

'Oh yes. I know what this is. It's the uniform of the 'Forêt et Eaux' (Forest and Waters).

'Are they soldiers?'

'No, not at all. They are guardians of the forest.'

'The thing is. We actually need two matching jackets. Have you any idea where I could find another?'

'You could ask the Mayor. He might lend you his.'

I rang up the Mairie the following day.

'I wonder if I could speak to the Mayor please.'

'Certainly Madame. May I ask what it is about?'

I hadn't expected this. 'Well, it's kind of a personal matter.'

The voice at the other end became noticeably suspicious.

'I can't put you through unless I have a reason.'

I really couldn't face trying to explain what I wanted on the phone, so I asked to make an appointment to see him.

The next day found me sitting on a plastic chair outside the Mayor's office trying to work out the least embarrassing way of asking the Mayor whether I could borrow a piece of his clothing.

I was ushered in. He was a new Mayor, quite young, with a dashing handlebar moustache.

'Madame, please take a seat. How may I help you?'

'Well, the thing is, we're putting on an opera…' I said falteringly. He had started taking notes. Suddenly I had visions of him asking about fire escapes and insurance and possibly even taxes!

'It's not a public performance,' I said hurriedly. 'It's private. Just for an invited audience. In fact, what we need are uniforms. I mean only jackets, we don't need trousers.' This was starting to sound pornographic. I could feel myself going bright red under his gaze. The Mayor has noticed my blushes (typical French male) and his eyes are starting to twinkle.

'I'm a friend of François Civreis. He suggested you might be able to help,' I added lamely.

Suddenly it was all fine. The mention of François, who was a positive bastion of the community, had opened all doors. The Mayor said he had two green jackets. He said we could borrow one of them for as long as we liked. He'd drop it round tomorrow.'

'You know where I live?'

Of course he did. He'd known who I was all along. He'd probably even been primed as to what I wanted by François.

Time passes and August is upon us. The jackets are now hanging up on the cast clothes rail. They're complete with smart black trousers and knee-high boots that should fit the singers provided Jane has given me the correct sizes.

The floor plan of the house with the bedroom allocations is pinned on the notice board in the hall. The list of recipes is on the pad in the kitchen. There's a casserole in the oven and the table is laid with eleven places. Peter, Pam and I are enjoying a last relaxed drink in the courtyard. The troupe is due to arrive at any minute. I have one eye on the driveway and one ear listening out for the phone because Claudia is also due to go into labour at any minute.

Of course I should be in Paris, doing my 'concerned mother' bit. This is after all my first grandchild. But I've got an opera to put on and she should have been a bit more careful nine months ago.

The cast arrive without us even hearing the cars on the gravel and suddenly the courtyard is full of people greeting each other. The new boys, Johnny and Hyalmar are introduced. Both are tall dark and good looking. But this is where the similarity ends, while Johnny is quiet and reserved, Hyalmar, who comes from Colombia, exudes Latin American machismo. As we sit down to dinner he deftly positions himself between the prettiest girls.

I'm having a bit of a problem with his name. Hyalmar – pronounced Yalma – is one of the least memorable names I've ever come across. Each time I turn to him to ask him to pass something or whether he'd like a second helping, I come up with a different version. It's getting really embarrassing. In the end I give up.

'Look, would you mind if I called you Fred?'

'Fred? No, I would be delighted,' he said with a flash of his perfect white teeth. So Fred he was, for the rest of the week.

The following morning we learn the significance of 'Pool Boy'. Nothing to do with billiards. Fred has set the first act of Cosi in and around the swimming pool. (I said that the pool would come in handy). There's a lawn that leads down to the pool. It even slopes so the seats will be raked. Don Alfonso (Fred) will be wearing a cream linen suit and lounging nonchalantly beside the pool. Nic's job is to stroll round the pool, skimming off any stray leaf.

It's lucky that Johnny and Hyalmar are such fine male specimens because their first appearance will be in swimwear. Their costumes consist of two pairs of swimming trunks, one turquoise, the other cerise. I don't think either suspected when they auditioned, that they would have to sing a duet while treading water.

All through that week I'm in a slightly tense state and jump every time the phone rings. At any moment Nick will be ringing to say the baby is on its way. And it rings a lot. It's never Nick though, the phone calls are all for Hyalmar.

I'm constantly answering it to find a breathless female voice saying: 'Pliz may I spik to Yalma?'

'Fred!' I shout out of the kitchen door for the umpteenth time.

'Can't you get him to ring her back?' asks Pam.

'What? To Colombia?'

It's getting very wearing. I ask Jane to have a word to Hyalmar about it. He solves the problem by buying an international phone card from the Post Office and calling whoever this poor female is at regular intervals. We wake in the night to hear the low droning of his voice on the phone at the weirdest times.

The rehearsals continue smoothly, for once Fred is well ahead in his schedule. Kitty, in particular, is absolutely word perfect and on the ball. When she and Donna sing together, I drop everything I'm doing and stop to listen. Johnny and Hyalmar are also a good team. Hyalmar in particular is hilarious at acting the jealous lover who has been duped by his girlfriend.

'How could she? I'm so handsome? Look at my feet, my legs, my....' He indicates parts of his body with Latin pride.

The news from Paris is that the baby may be late. I'm starting to feel the pressure is off when the phone calls start up again.

'Could I spik with Yalma pliz?'

'Fred!'

'I can't understand it,' I say to Pam. 'Jane told Yalma, I mean Fred, to tell that girl not to call him, he'd call her.'

'It's a different girl,' says Pam.

'Different! You mean there are two of them?'

'At least.'

'How do you know?'

'Jane told me.'

'Why am I the last to know anything?'

'You're the boss.'

'Who says?'

Pam rolls her eyes. 'Everyone!'

I go off and do some dutiful minion work just to prove to Pam how wrong she is. I unpack all Fred's costumes and hang them on hangers ready to be ironed. As I shake the clothes out one by one, 'Fifties skirts and tight shirts, waistcoats and socks his clever plan for clarifying the plot comes to light. The couples are colour coded: cerise and turquoise.

The night before the performance I get a call from Nick saying he's taking Claudia into the hospital, the labour pains have well and truly started. Talk about timing. I wait up by the phone. Eventually, the cast go to bed, each of the girls saying something excited or sympathetic as they leave. I stay up until around midnight but Nick texts me saying nothing will happen soon, I might as well go to bed – he'll let me know if there's any news.

I wake at seven the next morning with a start and reach for my mobile. There's a text on it, I was so exhausted I didn't hear it when it came in.

'Anouska' was born at four in the morning. Everything fine.

So it's a girl. Well, there's no reason why a girl can't have a blue cot is there?

Over breakfast Pam and I have a bet as to who will ask about the baby when they come down to breakfast. Every single girl asks for news and not a single male.

It's a beautiful day and we have a lot to celebrate. Peter opens a bottle of champagne at lunchtime and we each have a glass in spite of our 'no alcohol at lunch' rule. The day passes in a sort of haze and when the evening comes and the audience starts to arrive, I feel like an onlooker rather than a host. The glorious music gains a special poignancy with the knowledge of this new life that has entered the world.

Nature seems to be in league with the singers. The weather is on our side for once. The evening is warm and balmy. Swallows dip down and flit across the courtyard as the lovers exchange their vows. Even the cows in the neighbouring field seem to sense something special is going on, refraining from mooing and watching the action in the swimming pool with their bemused blank eyes.

According to Pam (who was there) the post-opera party was more outrageous than ever. A game of 'Truth or Dare' got rather out of hand with our pool cover getting ripped by a member of the cast who claimed he could 'walk on water'. Donna was dared into showing off two of her greatest assets. But Hyalmar was the one who did the star turn. Apparently he stripped off and did a 'bomb' into the swimming pool, landing hard on a sensitive part of his body and then went and sat down by himself very quietly.

'Served him right,' said Pam. 'Those two poor girls.'

Chapter Fifteen

There was to be no opera the following year. We had two weddings instead. And weddings have come a long way since Peter and I got married. It's not just the dress, the flowers, the speeches, the cake and the engraved invitations. Weddings these days have to be themed, with custom-made invitations, special music, gifts for the guests and entertainments. I perk up at the mention of entertainments - they wouldn't like a performance of 'The Marriage of Figaro' would they? I get a resounding: 'No'.

We consider getting Jane or one of the other sopranos over to sing. It's quite an expense for only one or two arias. But I've made friends with one of Opera Loki's competitors. A French/English couple have a daughter Lucie with a fine soprano voice. She's been trained in Italy and her father, on retiring from his architectural practice, runs an opera company called: 'Opera de Pôche' (Pocket Opera). They have a season in Moulins each summer performing, for the most part, rare operas with a small cast. We try to attend as many of them as we can. Opera companies in the philistine Allier need all the support they can get. Observing Opera de Pôche is a salutary lesson. Once a company becomes professional the balance sheet has to be - well - balanced. If you count the members of the audience and divide the price of the seats between the performers, it doesn't come to a lot.

We hire Lucie to sing at both weddings and I manage to rustle up a pianist – Alain, the piano teacher who had turned pages for us one year, to accompany her.

Claudia wants what she calls a 'Tess of the D'Urberville's Wedding'. I'm given the job of finding a suitably rustic horse and cart for the trip from the church to Gozinière. Conveniently, 'rustic' means we can borrow the benches and tables from the Mairie again. I already have all the tablecloths and white china for a hundred or so guests. Pam and I set to making table decorations with heads of lavendar and wheat ears. The date of 11th September means there's no way we can depend on the weather. I ring up marquee companies. I'm relieved to find that they are a lot more reasonable than in England. In fact, the fellow who runs the enterprise offers me a 'remise' (discount) if I'm willing to give his workers lunch. So French!

When the big day arrives, it's actually sunny. Peter's had a bumper crop of pumpkins and adds a final rustic touch to each table by using a pumpkin in which to skewer the table number. We strew the church aisle with lavendar which is crushed underfoot. For weeks afterwards the priest wonders why our little local church smells like a perfumerie.

Claudia and Nick go on a 'honeymoon' after the wedding - they're doing everything the wrong way round. They plan to leave Anouska - with me. I'm not too sure about having a baby plonked on me. Claudia points out that I can't do worse than her. I know something about babies - I've had two, whereas she's a complete novice.

One of the spin-off effects of this wedding is that we find the amazing M.Sennepin - 'Traiteur'. Claudia had put her foot down about Pam and I doing the catering. There is no way our cooking would be up to the standard of her Parisian guests – her wedding catering had to be done by professionals.

Peter and I went to visit this 'wizard of the kitchen', in an office situated behind his shop where a mouth-watering selection of his 'Delicatessen' was on display. I led Peter past 'feulletté de saumon', 'paté aux morilles' and glossy lobster surrounded by a supporting cast of king prawns. M. Sennepin brushed away all our worries with a wave of his hand. What about refrigeration? He would bring his refrigerated lorry to our back door. How would he manage with my cooker? He had his own, powered by his own generator. What about serving staff? How many did we want? He had a staff of waiters on call. How much would all this cost?

When we worked it out, the sum didn't seem to come to much more than if we'd cooked it ourselves. We selected a menu we thought would pass Parisian scrutiny. It included a main course of quail, boned and stuffed with fresh figs.

'You're going to have your hands full, boning a hundred and twenty quail,' I said jokingly. He just nodded. 'It'll take a little time.'

I'd assumed he'd get boned quail from the Far East or something, but 'no' apparently he prepared them all himself.

Of course we used him as the official caterer for all our operas after that. He got into the spirit of the whole thing, absorbing information about the plot and the location of the action and suggesting dishes that would tie in with the opera. Most memorable of his dishes was a vast, succulent paella which he made for 'Carmen' and a menu for 'La Cenerentola' (Rossini's Cinderella) which was predominately pink.

Leo's wedding takes place in December. Peter and I have to do all the legal business for the couple as they are both busy working in the U.K. I discover that it's way more complicated – and expensive – than getting a licence in England. There are endless forms to fill in and we have to get a translation of both Leo and Charlie's passports by a certified legal translator. We pay fifty euros per passport for this 'expert' to translate 'Date' and 'Place of Birth'.

I'm staggered at the commitment of Leo and Charlie's friends who are willing to come all the way to Central France for a wedding. We can't put them all up, so most of them stay in Moulins and we hire a bus to take them back and forth. We decide to have the wedding feast in the attic. Remembering Figaro's magical garden of a couple of years back, Pam and I hang yew branches from the rafters and thread tiny fairy lights through them. We're just adding the finishing touches when M. Aubertin arrives at the front door dragging the biggest bunch of mistletoe I've ever seen – it's at least a metre in diameter. We haul it up in the hallway where it forms the centre-piece of the house.

It's a totally different wedding from Claudia's. We take out the double doors opening up all the rooms into each other and have a firelit disco. The evening ends with fireworks and a huge bonfire on the lawn. There's no horse and cart for Leo. We wave the couple off in a vintage Citroën DS – Charlie's favourite car.

The next day I wander round the house picking up things and putting them down, wondering where to start in the chaos. I lean out of the dormer window for a breath of fresh air. The date of the house is inscribed above my head in the wooden lintel 1758. Next year will be 2008 – exactly two hundred and fifty years since the house was built.

I go down to find Peter who has had to get out the trailer in order to cart the bottles to the bottle bank.

'Guess what's happening next year?'

'We haven't got another daughter to marry, have we?'

'It'll be the two hundred and fiftieth anniversary of this house.'

'Ye-es.'

'We need to mark it in some way. Celebrate.'

Peter heaved the last box of empties into the trailer and shoved the tail-gate closed.

'What about Figaro? I mean, doing it properly this time. Getting all the audience to come in costume. Having an 18th Century feast.'

Peter got into the car and turned on the ignition.

'I'll just get rid of this lot of bottles first.'

Chapter Sixteen

I'd like to end by describing the actual performance of 'The Marriage of Figaro'. But like fireworks on television and sex in books – you really have to be there for it to be anything like the real thing.

So you'll have to content yourself with the preparations, slips, spills and shenanigans back stage. These actually started a long time back when I was back in London, visiting Leo and Charlie, ostensibly to make curtains for their new house.

I was in the haberdashery department of Peter Jones buying Rufflette tape when I just happened to take a peek inside the Simplicity Pattern Book and found a brilliant pattern for an 18th Century dress. It would take a lot of material but there is the Marché St Pierre...

I rang Pam with the good news.

'How many of these 'Simple' dresses are you thinking of making?'

'Well, there's one for me and one for Leo and another for Claudia. And I'll have to do something for Peter.'

'And one for me and one for Connie.'

'Ummm.'

'And what about all the other guests?'

'They don't have to come as aristocrats. They can come as peasants, tarts, priests or nuns...'

'Sounds a bit kinky.'

'Or shepherds or woodchoppers, or what are those people who hole up alone in caves?'

'Hermits?'

'They'll only need hair shirts.'

On the way back to Gozinière, I spend a night with Claudia and Nick (and Anouska) in Paris. I find time to go up to the Marché St Pierre, just to take a look at what they've got.

They have metres and metres of gorgeous satin for a knock-down price. I have my pattern with me. I need ten metres per dress. I select three different colours and watch the glossy metres being measured out. When my parcel is packed, it's so heavy I have to leave it with the assistant and go and buy a suitcase on wheels to cart it home.

Back at Gozinière I unwrap the parcel and lay the fabric out on the dining table, checking the metres like a miser counting his money.

'What's all that for?' asks Peter, as he passes through the room.

'Our costumes for the Figaro evening.'

'I'm not sure it's going to happen.'

'Why not?'

'I've had an email from Fred. He was really apologetic but he said he can't spare the time to direct this summer. He's got a part in the 'Pirates of Penzance'. It's a big break for him.'

This was a blow. I couldn't envisage an opera without Fred.

'He says we can use his libretto anyway. Jane's trying to find another director.'

'What happens if she can't?'

'We can't do an opera without a director.'

I'm not going to be put off. I cut out the first dress anyway. There seems to be an awful lot of material in the skirt. I study the pattern wondering if I've gone wrong somewhere and realise that the hips have to be padded out. Once this is done, I try it on. It's so full I have to go sideways to get through a doorway.

The blokes - Peter, Nick and Charlie - will need costumes too. I sort through my hoard of braids and bindings and come across an Indian sari I'd completely forgotten about - a Christmas present that Marjorie had bought accidentally in an auction – she didn't have her reading glasses with her at the time. It's lovely: turquoise blue with a thick border of gold embroidery, I'd never been able to think what to do with it. A week or so later Marjorie's auction mistake has begun a new life as an Eighteenth Century jacket. The gold embroidery is running down the front and makes two heavy turn-backs on the sleeves. Peter is inside this lot turning from side to side, admiring his reflection in the mirror.

'I'll need a shirt of course.'

'And a lace stock and stockings.'

'Stockings!'

'Well, long socks.'

'Hmmm.'

'It'll be awful if we have to cancel because we don't have a director.'

'I've been thinking about that.'

'Oh?'

'How about Malcolm?'

Malcolm was a neighbor - a documentary film maker who had, in the past, worked as a drama director for the BBC.

'Do you think he could direct an opera?'

'I don't see why not, especially if we have a good musical director.'

'But we don't yet.' Roland couldn't make it this year either.

'Do you think he'll want to do it?'

'Direct Figaro? I should think he'll jump at the opportunity.'

'What about the singers? How will they feel being directed by someone so much older than them.'

'I'll ask Jane.'

Jane said she'd be happy with any director we were happy with. She would concentrate on finding a really good pianist/repetiteur.

Now all we had to do was ask Malcolm.

I cooked one of his favourite meals with Tarte Tatin for pudding flamed with Calvados. As we finished our meal, Peter poured Malcolm a glass of Drambuie (his favourite tipple).

'So Malcolm. Listen, I'm about to offer you a brilliant opportunity.'

(Still the smooth old ad. man).

'Oh?'

'How would you like to direct The Marriage of Figaro?'

'You mean here?'

We both nodded.

'Why can't Fred do it?'

'He's pulled out. He's got a part in a Gilbert and Sullivan run he can't afford to refuse.'

'I see.'

'You wouldn't have to stay here. But of course you'll have all your meals with us. Swim in the pool. It should be fun.'

'And to cap it all, it's unpaid,' I added.

'Oh, in that case you've talked me into it,' said Malcolm.

Jane found an excellent pianist - Tim Short. He went on to become Opera Loki's Musical Director and also a great friend. He proved to be indefatigable. He was happy to play at all the rehearsals, accompany soloists between rehearsals and would even leave the table mid-meal to entertain us with hysterically naff renderings of vintage musicals. Malcolm would join him, breaking into song.

Tim always gave a hundred per cent to his playing. One year during a slightly doomed performance of 'Die Enfuhrung' (Yes, inevitably, we did have some less successful evenings) when a freak storm knocked out the speakers and the singers couldn't hear the piano, Tim played on relentlessly, despite his fingers slipping on the wet keys. Like the string quartet while the Titanic went down – nothing could put him off his stroke.

The good news was that Donna had agreed to come back to sing the Countess. Jane had cast a new soprano - Ellie Moran to play Susanna, who she said we'd absolutely love. We had a new Count too, Daniel Roddick – I looked up his C.V. on the internet – he was gorgeous. Jane was going to sing the love-sick youth, Cherubino. And there was a surprising new addition - an assistant stage manager – a chap called Paul Gray. I rang Jane to ask if he was really necessary, Kate generally managed with help from me and Pam.

'He's also going to sing Antonio - the gardener.'

'But can't someone else do that if you double up?'

'He won't need a bed.'

'No? Why not?''

'He'll be in mine, if that's all right.'

'Uh.Huh!'

As June turns into July I happily sew my way through yards and yards of satin. The dining table has been turned into a cutting table. Jaqueline moans and frets over the threads and scraps littering the floor. But the dresses are taking shape. As each one is finished, I hang it from the light fitting in the music room – they're far too long to go in a cupboard. The Music Room soon looks as if some mass execution of aristocrats has taken place. Not far from the truth as my researches into the history of the house are starting to reveal.

The cast's costumes have thankfully been taken care of. Jane has found a theatrical costume hire company who are willing to lend us the lot for a reasonable price as long as they use them for their subsequent performances in the U.K.

Jane has a couple of venues lined up for further performances that hopefully will make a profit to share between the singers. It's the first step towards making Opera Loki a more viable company. Peter is making headway in getting the company charitable status.

Pam returns to France after a trip to help Connie move into sheltered accommodation. She eyes my needlework with professional scepticism.

'It's a good thing you're not making the cast's costumes. These wouldn't hold out for more than a performance or two.'

Later when I examine the professional costumes, I can see what she means. The 18th Century dresses are boned and laced and interlined and basically have an infrastructure designed to support soprano bosoms.

Malcolm has been over to discuss the staging. I take him out to the box hedges and point out where he could have the entrances and exits for the final scene in the garden. He's unimpressed, for him the all-important thing is the acoustics. He wants to stage the whole opera in the courtyard.

'And I want raked seating,' he says as an afterthought.

'But we've always managed with the folding chairs from the Mairie, they're easy to cart around for different scenes.'

'We won't need to cart them around if it's all set in the courtyard,' he points out.

I try a few more excuses but he's adamant.

That night Peter and I feel despondent. Malcolm is doing us a terrific favour directing the opera, we don't feel we can refuse this request.

'There must be someone in the area who can loan us raked

seating.'

'We could ask the Footsbarn,' suggests Peter.

The Footsbarn is a local theatre company who give performances in a massive, portable big top. Their versions of classic plays by Shakespeare, Gogol or Molière are a fascinating combination of clowning, poetry and music, often performed in several languages simultaneously. They created a magical 'Midsummer Night's Dream, that was performed in Stratford on Avon.

'I could ring them and ask.'

They didn't turn a hair at my request. 'We're all off to China for the summer,' the voice at the other end said, so we won't need it ourselves. You're welcome to borrow the seating.'

'How much would you charge to hire it out?'

'We won't need paying but you'll have to send someone to collect it and return it.'

As ever, we found people we've asked to help with Opera Loki have been incredibly generous. All we had to find now was a method of transporting it. Dennis, the friend who'd originally introduced us to the Footsbarn, solved this problem. He had a lorry, not in its first youth, it had 400,000 kms on the clock, but it was still roadworthy - just. He offered to pick up the decking from the Footsbarn and help erect it. An offer I snapped up. The last time Peter put anything together it came from Ikea and it still has one of the pieces glued in upside down.

It turned out to be a nightmare to erect. Dennis, his son, M.Aubertin and Peter all chipped in. The decking was made of oak and incredibly heavy. It was just as well we weren't giving a paying performance because we would never have got it through 'Health and Safety'.

So now we had raked seating. We had M.Sennepin standing by to provide the dinner. All the beds were ready and the freezer already had a couple of meals stowed away. All we needed now was the cast.

All thirteen of them arrived safely. No one missed the plane or the train or lost their passport or luggage. Peter and a friend collected them from the station and came back with the trailer piled high with baggage.

'Phew, the new Susanna's a bit of all right,' he commented.

Ellie was blonde and blue-eyed with a perfect peaches and cream complexion. Dan, who was to play the Count, more than lived up to his photo. Then there was Russell - a Don Basilio with a wonderful Welsh accent and a wicked grin. A girl called Emma who towered over him, well in fact over everyone, had been cast as his 'wife' Marcellina – this had comic potential.

And then of course, there was Paul Gray. I watched as he helped unload the trailer. Would he do for Jane? She felt like a daughter by now, Paul had to pass our scrutiny.

We were becoming accustomed to new casts arriving. There was always the rather subdued first dinner when they were all being incredibly polite and helpful, the first breakfast, when you discover who are the keen ones, up for a run before breakfast or having a refreshing early swim and those who arrive still half-asleep. Tim Short, the pianist, was one of the latter, late most mornings, mainly because he could sleep through anything - people walking through his room, alarm clocks - three of them - even the wet flannel treatment. Then there's the first lunch when they're being abstemious and not piling their plates too high. By the second dinner, they are starting to relax. Bottles of wine are disappearing at the rate of knots and the speed of eating has accelerated as they compete for second helpings.

By the third day, they become the noisy, irreverent bunch who seem to have known each other, and us, for weeks. They're teasing Pam and sending Peter up and even being quite cheeky to Malcolm.

The weather is hot and the skies are a clear forget-me-knot blue. They're getting off-stage entertainments down to a fine art. They've put up the badminton net and are sorting out a tournament. There's a darts match going on in the barn and the swimming pool is hosting a noisy game of water polo.

Malcolm wants a traditional 18th Century production (thank goodness!). Kate and I sort through the furniture and props. Malcolm selects a screen, a little walnut writing table, a chaise longue and the console mirror for the Countess's bedroom. I have bought an ancient wooden dark lantern for Barbarina's search for the missing 'pin'. Since we can't use the box hedges for the final act, Kate and Paul construct a shrubbery out of hardboard. I'm given the job of painting this. I bring my 'shrubbery' out into the courtyard so that I can listen to the rehearsal while I work.

Dan and Ellie are really convincing as the Count and Susanna. I watch Dan patting his knee invitingly – an invitation Ellie accepts perhaps almost too readily. I'll have to talk to Malcolm about it. Emma is brilliant as Marcellina, she has a voice and a half – big enough to reach the upper circle in The Royal Opera House with ease.

Paul as Antonio, the gardener is not doing quite so well. I can hear Jane in the music room tutoring him. Over and over again he sings;

'Oh my Lord…my Lord…. Please will you listen to me?'

And she's stopped him. He's out of time and he's also out of breath. They start again. I'm so used to hearing the singers performing effortlessly, it's easy to forget how difficult it actually is. They have to remember their lines, they have to be in time and perfectly on pitch. They have to know when to breathe. While doing this, they also need to be in the right place, making exactly the right action. Add the other variables, such as trying to sing your part while two or three other singers are singing a different version of the melody and you wonder how on earth they ever do it.

'Oh my Lord… My Lord…. Please will you listen to me?'

Paul has had no singing training. He's being incredibly patient with Jane and so is Jane with him. This match seems promising.

In fact the whole house has taken on a kind of rosy glow as if the spirit of the opera's 'one perfect day' has taken over. I catch Emma moving her bedding into another room. She's been sharing with Ellie and for some reason this isn't working out. I help her relocate in a through-room off the bathroom.

Pam, as ever, is the one to get the lowdown.

'Haven't you noticed?'

'Noticed what?'

'Dan and Ellie.'

'Umm, I wondered if they were overdoing it.'

'It isn't acting.'

'Oh-hh!'

Ellie and Dan are a joy to have around. Ellie positively radiates happiness and Dan looks pretty pleased with himself. I think we're all enjoying a vicarious frisson of their romance. I tot up Gozinière's success stories: Claudia and Nick. Leo and Charlie. Jane and Paul. Ellie and Dan. I always said there was something magical about this house.

Malcolm has come up with a fresh demand. He wants a dog to accompany the Count when he returns from hunting in Act 2. Hubert, a new French friend and committed anglophile, has offered to lend us James Marmaduke Clarence. Despite his anglophile name, James Marmaduke is nothing like a British hound. He's a massive stag-hunting dog that stands nearly a metre high. But he's actually a pet and extremely gentle. When Hubert turns up with him for a rehearsal, he also brings an enormous dish of cassoulet, big enough to feed the entire cast - plus a dead hare.

'What's this for?'

'I thought if the Count comes back from hunting, he'd better have something to show for it.'

The dead hare is stiff. Pam takes charge of it. She comes across Peter storing potatoes in the potting shed.

'What are you doing with that?'

'Hanging it.'

'Isn't it dead already?' he goes off laughing at his own joke.

She rolls her eyes.

The night of the performance arrives. We have to get into costume as well as the cast. This adds extra pressure to the whole occasion. There are last minute panics as Leo and Claudia get laced up. They've swapped frocks which means Claudia's dress is too loose. She wants Pam to take some tucks in it. I have an antique white lawn baby dress for Anouska – she's grown somewhat since I bought it and we literally have to force her head through into it.

I've bought Peter a pair of outsize blue tights to wear under his costume. They keep falling down and I tell him to wear his underpants over them. It's not a good look. But somehow we're all in costume by the time the first guests arrive.

Malcolm turns up looking fantastic, dressed in an Eighteenth Century costume complete with powdered wig. He's going to use it afterwards in the documentary he's making about Adam Smith.

The guests arrive in a miscellaneous hotch-potch of costumes. Graham, one of Peter's clients, comes in a magnificent scarlet cardinal's robe. We have an Eighteenth Century judge with a proper judge's wig. Françoise Civreis is dressed as peasant and François has got the century wrong – he's actually in a Sixteenth Century outfit of doublet and hose. We have a Lord Nelson and an Emma Hamilton, a couple of soldiers in uniform, several vagrants and numerous tarts in various states of undress. We haven't got a hermit yet but there's still time.

The house stands bathed in evening sunlight which flatters its wrinkles and blemishes, which it can be forgiven for since it's celebrating its two hundred and fiftieth birthday.

Gozinière looks terrific with all these people in costume milling round it. I herd the ones who are in disgrace for not making an effort, to the far side of the drive and we have a load of pictures taken.

I've given Peter a brief historical run-down to include in his speech. I've warned him not to dwell too long on the injustices of the Revolution, we have a load of 'lefties in the audience but 'Liberté, Egalité and Fraternité seem to be the rule this evening, particularly Fraternité – I can see Christian the vet, and committed Socialist, having a laugh with the biggest land-owner in the Allier.

All the things that could go wrong, don't. It doesn't rain. The Footsbarn's seating doesn't collapse. Nobody forgets their lines – or props. It's all going like clockwork until the Count's entrance with James Marmaduke. There's a pause. Tim improvises a little variation on a theme to fill the silence.

And then all hell lets loose. There's a lot of yowling and barking and fur flying.

I heard from Pam afterwards what happened off-stage. James Marmaduke, who had played his part immaculately in the rehearsal, had taken one look at the audience and had a fit of stage-fright. Pam, with great presence of mind, remembered the hare. She rushed to the potting shed and retrieved it for the Count. The Count hung it over his shoulder and made his entrance, followed by J.M. nose-first. Boris, one of our aristochats, also got scent of it. J.M. and Boris met mid-stage. Not sure who came off worst - probably the hare.

Once they'd got everything back up the right way and the audience had settled down again, the performance continued flawlessly. I was getting nervous for Paul. I just hoped an audience wouldn't have the effect it had had on James Marmaduke. Paul made his entrance carrying a broken flowerpot with a geranium in it. The geranium was shaking like a leaf. In the background Cherubino's lips were moving following Antonio's every note. But he did it. He was spot on and got a well-deserved round of applause.

The performance went by far too fast. As the last magical notes of that final quartet come to an end, I was struck by a feeling of sadness. Suddenly it was all over. I'd had my performance of Figaro and it would never happen again. Now, I had nothing to look forward to.

It wasn't just the opera, but all the preparations – all the cooking and sewing, all the tears and laughter, all the trials and turmoil of a house full of youth and music.

And with the lightening speed at which memory can move, my brain went into action-replay to how we've arrived at this moment. I remembered the first shy entrance of the troupe from Bedfordshire Youth Opera. Then the chaos of our years of renovation, and further back too - to the finding of the house even. All of these seemed to culminate in this one last fleeting moment.

When the last guest had gone, Pam found me blubbing in the back kitchen.

'What's up?'

'It's just that it's all over. Fred won't direct any more because he wants to act. And they're all getting professional and married and they'll be having babies and need to earn money for rent and mortgages and...' (pause for noisy nose-blowing) 'It's going to be far too expensive. So this will be our last opera ever.'

Postscript

Of course Figaro wasn't our last opera. But we had to pull up our socks and become more professional. Opera Loki is now a registered charity. We have a Board of Directors and a proper Treasurer who has sorted out the finances.

We have formulated our official aims which are:

'To help young singers develop their careers' and 'To bring opera to a wider audience'.

Since that second performance of The Marriage of Figaro, Opera Loki has staged the following operas:

Die Enfuhrung aus dem Serail

As mentioned earlier, this was not one of our best. Die Enfuhrung is known to be an opera with a curse on it, and it lived up to its reputation with everything including the weather turning against us. Its one redeeming feature was that Russell played Pedrillo on the insistence that we include his comic aria about the donkey - which was hilarious.

Carmen

We insisted that Jane sang the title role. She made a smouldering Carmen and Dan made an extremely dashing Escamillo in one of the costumes I'm most proud of making (could whoever has it at present, please return it?).

La Cenerentola

Fred wanted to direct this with the names of the two ugly sisters changed to Claudia and Leonora. In fact, that summer he landed a choice part in the U.K. so we had a new director and the girls were let off this embarrassment. Pam and I recycled our 18th Century dresses for the ugly sisters and Cinderella. In spite of what Pam said they held together for quite a number of performances, actually.

The Barber of Seville

We found a new director, Rae Leaver, to take Fred's place and a new lead soprano, Gillian McIlwraith who played Rosina. She had a fabulous voice and could certainly turn up the volume. Russell played Count Almaviva with comic panache particularly in his drunken soldier disguise (type-casting?). Pam and I made all the costumes and loved every minute of it (at least I did).

La Traviata

By this time we felt our singers were mature enough to tackle Verdi. Auditions were held in London and we discovered a wonderful new soprano: Luci Briginshaw, who has sung with Opera Loki ever since. Not only does Luci have an exquisite voice but she's also an excellent actress. The tissues were out as the final act came to a close.

Rigoletto

Luci played Gilda – a totally convincing 16 year old, in contrast to her sophisticated Violetta. And we found an extremely fine Rigoletto in Oliver Gibbs. The cast was too numerous to detail here. The best way to catch up with Opera Loki is to see it live. Check the website for details: www.operaloki.com

La Bohème

At the time of going to print, La Bohème has not yet been cast. Watch this space.

Opera Loki's aims and successes:

Over the years we've come to terms with the fact that as our singers mature, they will go on to professional careers and we will lose them. This is a bonus not a threat.

Cast members have moved on to sing at the Royal Opera House, Glyndebourne, ENO, WNO and English National Touring Opera. One cast member joined the Jette Parker Young Artists' Programme at the Royal Opera House in 2010 and in 2011 Kitty Whateley was the winner of the Kathleen Ferrier Award.

Kitty Whateley
Kitty is among Opera Loki's major successes. After winning the Kathleen Ferrier Award, she joined ENO with whom she now sings leading roles. Peter, Pam and I made a pilgrimage up to York to hear her sing Rosina in the Barber of Seville. It was difficult to reconcile the gorgeous slender girl on stage with the cuddly Kitty we'd known at Gozinière – but once that voice of hers rang out we recognised her instantly.

Donna Loomens
Donna became Donna Lennard and has a baby Scarlett. She did get into Music College and now is a professional singer full-time.

Nic Gibney
Nic finished his degree at Guildford School of Musical Theatre and landed his first big role touring with The Rocky Horror Show. This was followed up by Evita. His latest photo shows that gorgeous blue-eyed Adonis with a beard – gosh Nic!

Fred Broom
Fred also graduated from Guildford and has starred in many roles in Gilbert and Sullivan. He's also played Mr Toad in The Wind and the Willows. In his current biog he admits he still weighs in at 18 stone (Fred honestly!) He compensates for this by being an excellent musician, playing: Gd8 Piano, Violin, Viola, Gd5 Bass, Double Bass.

Jane Mabbitt
Jane married Paul, so she's now Jane Gray. (Or Little Gray Mabbitt as we call her) They have a baby – Bertie. My prediction that they would all give up when they had babies didn't come true. We are looking forward to her directing future Opera Loki performances.

Tyler Clarke
Tyler was winner of the 2009 Les Auzriales Opera Trust Prize. He studied at the RCM International Opera School followed by the Georg Solti Academia di Bel Canto and National Opera Studio. He made his ENO debut as Liverotto in Lucrezia Borgia and also sang Count Almaviva in The Barber of Seville for ENO.

Daniel Grice
Daniel recently played Schaunard in La Bohème at the Royal Opera House. He also starred as Papageno in The Magic Flute with WNO.

Kate Bazin
Kate became a teaching fellow at King's College London and has married. She and Honoré have just had their first baby so we have had to find a new Stage Manager to fill in.

Dan Roddick
Dan has continued his double career – as he puts it 'working in private equity by day and moonlighting as an opera singer by night'. He and Russell have been taken up by our friends Carl and Veronica to give oratorio performances in Perigourd.

Ellie Moran
Ellie went on to sing Mimi in the Opera Up Close award winning production of La Bohème. Sadly, after three or so years, she and Dan split up. She hasn't come back to La Gozinière because she said she just can't bear the memories.

Russell Painter
Russell vies with Nic in the role of the La Gozinière pet. He is carving out a career for himself particularly in roles where humour is involved. He is also (in his own words) a lover of real ale, a fully qualified safari park tour guide, a keen walker and a Monday evening circuit training fanatic.

Gillian McIlwraith
Gill has sung and covered roles for companies such as Opera North, Glyndebourne, Garsington, Bampton Classical Opera, Mid Wales Opera, Castleward and Swansea city Opera.

Luci Briginshaw
You can see Luci singing at Covent Garden on You Tube. Courageously she sings as a street performer. Opera Loki's aim is to get such girls off the street and into the Opera Houses where they belong.

Rae Leaver
Rae took over from Fred as Opera Loki's long term director. Her directing innovations included a 1940's Traviata in which, the Baron (Violetta's protector) is a Nazi sympathiser and Alfredo's family is Jewish. And a Victorian travelling player's version of 'Rigoletto'.

Tim Short
Tim was our indefatigable pianist for five or more performances. He became a great friend and brought his actress girlfriend to visit. He now divides his time between playing piano on major Cruise liners and using the money he's earned to learn to fly jumbo jets, and he's now qualified as a pilot..

Nick Fletcher
Nick took over from Tim as Opera Loki's musical director. He did a sterling job with the difficult Verdi choruses earning accolades from the audience and critics. He's leaving us in 2015 to take up a post in the U.S.A

There are many more extremely valued members of the cast. Too many to do justice to in this book. So I've concentrated on the people who were involved in those first performances at Gozinière.

An enormous thank you to everyone else. Maybe I could include you in a sequel?

Opera Loki's Future

Over the past few years we have developed the Opera Loki French season. Besides the performance at La Gozinière, they also have performed: At Belabre in the Creuse generously hosted by Martin Gordon. At Les Vieux Melays - Allier hosted by Marc and Laurence Terray And this year we will have a fourth performance at Joel and Catherine Boutrolle's magnificently restored Chateau de Romenay.

Opera Loki has held London performances in Highgate, Vauxhall, Wimbledon and Great Malden. They also go on tour to Alton and Warwick. In early 2015 they performed Rigoletto at The Hurlingham Club and later La Bohème at the Oriental Club, both in London.

We are grateful to the many sponsors and the generous donations that have been given to Opera Loki.

Also to the people who have so generously given their time such as Pam Line and Liz Cassie (dresser per excellence) Dennis Harrap, venerable transporter and erecter of raked seating (he's due a diploma in chair moving). Malcolm Hossick who apart from directing 'The Marriage of Figaro' for us, also made a film at La Gozinière. To see the house in the flesh, order Malcolm's film of Ibsen's 'Ghosts' from Academy films via Amazon.

We'd also like to thank the people who have so kindly chipped in with transporting: the cast, piano, lighting and costumes. And lending: their rooms for auditions, raked seating, cloaks, ruffs, boots, walking sticks, hats, masks, wigs, fans, hundreds of chairs, a hunting dog, a punt, a vintage lorry and a life-size stuffed cow.

A BIG THANK YOU

Our thanks go to everyone who has purchased this book, the profits from it will go towards future Opera Loki performances.

We are most grateful to all those in France and the UK who have made generous donations. If you would like to make a donation to Opera Loki, please contact either Lynne Hill (Treasurer) on lynne.hunter@rocketmail.com or Peter Bear (President) on p.bear@wanadoo.fr ; or you can send a cheque, payable to 'Opera Loki' to Lynne Hill, The Granary, Honey Lane, Selborne, Hampshire, UK. GU34 3BY.

For information about future Opera Loki performances, see their website: www.operaloki.com

If you – or any of your friends – have an appropriate venue and would like to stage an Opera Loki performance, please contact Peter Bear (p.bear@wanadoo.fr) for the Terms and Conditions.

Another book for you to enjoy

'LOST & FOUND'
By Chloe Rayban

If you've enjoyed reading "How to Knit an Opera" you might also enjoy reading Chloe Rayban's latest novel "Lost & Found", based on the turbulent history of La Gozinière and interweaving an intriguing love story.

It's published digitally by Endeavour Press and can be downloaded on amazon.co.uk or amazon.com.

It is also available in paperback from: www.lulu.com

Praise for Lost & Found:
'A perfect blend of romance and self-discovery' - Holly Kinsella, bestselling author of 'Uptown Girl'

Chloe Rayban is the author of over 20 books for teenagers. She has been short-listed for the Guardian Children's Fiction Prize twice and the Carnegie Medal. Her books have been translated into many different languages and are sold all over the world. She lives in London and France. 'Lost and Found' is her first adult novel.

Endeavour Press is the UK's leading independent publisher of digital books.